A Middle School Plan for Students with College-Bound Dreams

This book belongs to:

_____

College class of:

_____

A Middle School Plan for Students with College-Bound Dreams

MYCHAL WYNN

RISING SUN
PUBLISHING

Other books by the author:

A High School Plan for Students with College-Bound Dreams
A High School Plan for Students with College-Bound Dreams: Workbook
A Middle School Plan for Students with College-Bound Dreams: Workbook
A Senior School Plan for Bermudian Students with College-Bound Dreams
A Middle School Plan for Bermudian Students with College-Bound Dreams
A Middle School Plan for Bermudian Students with College-Bound Dreams: Workbook
Don't Quit
Empowering African-American Males (book and workbook)
Follow Your Dreams: Lessons That I Learned in School
Ten Steps to Helping Your Child Succeed in School (book and workbook)
Test of Faith
The Eagles who Thought They were Chickens (book, teacher's guide, and student activity book)

A Middle School Plan for Students with College-Bound Dreams
Second Edition
Printing   1

ISBN-13: 978-1-880463-67-3
ISBN-10: 1-880463-67-9
Copyright © 2005 Mychal Wynn
Copyright © 2005 Rising Sun Publishing, Inc.

Disclaimers: The author, Mychal Wynn, or any of the content contained in this book should not in any way be construed as a representation or warranty that the reader will achieve this result. This book is designed to provide accurate and authoritative information in regard to the subject matter covered. The author and the publisher, however, make no representation or warranties of any kind with regard to the completeness or accuracy of the contents herein and accept no liability of any kind.

The poem, "A Pledge to Myself" is from the book, *Don't Quit*, copyright 1990 by Mychal Wynn.

Credits:
Cover design by Mychal Wynn.
Student Photographs taken by Mychal Wynn.
Stock Photographs by Fotosearch.
Photographic touch up by Jennifer Gibbs.

Reference sources for style and usage: *The New York Public Library Writer's Guide to Style and Usage.* Copyright 1994 by The New York Public Library and the Stonesong Press, Inc., and the *APA Stylebook 2004* by the Associated Press.

RISING SUN
PUBLISHING

P.O. Box 70906
Marietta, GA 30007-0906
770.518.0369/800.524.2813
FAX 770.587.0862
E-mail: info@rspublishing.com
Web site: http://www.rspublishing.com

Printed in the United States of America.

Acknowledgments

I would like to acknowledge my wife, Nina, who, as a wife, mother, confidant, and business partner has greatly contributed to the ideas contained within this book. She has put into practice the strategies as she has successfully guided our older son's oftentimes complex and frequently frustrating journey from preschool through high school, into his acceptance via Early Decision into Amherst College. She has also inspired, enlightened, and encouraged other children and their families along their parallel journeys from preschool into college.

I would also like to thank my nieces, Tishandra deCourcy and Kymberly McKay, for their efforts in ensuring that this workbook is usable and doable for any student in any situation; Dr. Glenn Bascome for his editorial assistance; Dr. Melvyn Bassett, Ms. LeeAnn Simmons, and Deana Ingham for their critical insight; and Dr. Genevieve Shephard and the staff at Tom Bradley Elementary School in Los Angeles, California, who are giving their students a jump start on their futures by creating a college-bound culture.

Lastly, I would like to thank my mother and father who encouraged, sacrificed, and inspired me to become the first college graduate in our family.

Dedication

This book is dedicated to my sons, Mychal-David and Jalani, the thousands of students and parents I meet each year who have college-bound hopes and aspirations, and to those who sacrifice each day on behalf of students and their dreams.

Table of Contents

About the Author

Mychal Wynn was an unlikely college-bound student, having been expelled from Chicago's De La Salle Catholic High School and barely earning enough credits to graduate from Chicago's Du Sable High School. Even more miraculous was his being accepted into Northeastern University, at the time, the largest private university in the United States and the only college that he applied to. Without a mentor to advise him or the benefit of the type of college-planning that is outlined in this book, he had not taken the required courses to be admitted directly from high school into college. He received a *conditional acceptance*—conditional upon his taking and passing classes in Physics and Calculus (courses which were not offered at his high school). As a result of his not having the opportunity to take the necessary classes in high school, his college dreams were deferred as he was required to enroll in Chicago's Kennedy-King Junior College for one semester in the fall of 1974. While working the night shift at the U.S. Post Office from 10:30 p.m. until 2:30 a.m., he took classes in Physics and Calculus during the day, receiving an 'A' in Physics and a 'B' in Calculus.

In January 1975, he boarded his first airplane as he flew from Chicago, Illinois to Boston, Massachusetts where he entered into the Northeastern University College of Engineering. In June 1979, Mychal Wynn became his family's first college graduate, receiving his Bachelor of Science degree. This once unlikely college-bound student was a highly-recruited college graduate and has worked for such multinational companies as IBM and the Transamerica Corporation. In 1985, he and his wife, Nina, founded Rising Sun Publishing, where his wife serves as the Publisher and Chief Executive Officer and he serves as the principal trainer and Chief Financial Officer.

Mr. Wynn is living his dreams as a husband, father, entrepreneur, and author of over 16 books. He, his wife, Nina, and their two sons, Mychal-David and Jalani, reside in Georgia.

Introduction

When our older son was in the first grade we were called in for a parent-teacher conference. His teacher was concerned with his lack of concentration and his continual failure to complete his class work. As an example, she showed my wife and me worksheets that were completely blank, with the exception of stick people running up the right side of the page, stick airplanes flying across the page, and stick people parachuting down the left side of the page. My wife and I, in collaboration with his classroom teacher, developed a series of strategies to not only get our son to complete more of his class work but to provide greater opportunities to nurture his passion for "stick people."

Over the ensuing years, my wife and I developed the type of comprehensive plan contained in this book, the accompanying *workbook*, and the high school books, to help nurture our son's passion for drawing while ensuring that he had a well-rounded and rigorous academic schedule that provided a broad range of college opportunities. Subsequently, he not only had a choice of some of the country's top-ranked art schools like the Savannah College of Art and Design and the Art Center College of Design in Pasadena, California, he was a candidate for such Ivy League schools as Yale and Dartmouth, and was admitted into his first-choice, Amherst College.

Our younger son is now in middle school and well into his college-bound plan. As a fifth-grader he visited several colleges and proclaimed, "I want to go to Yale" after listening to an admissions officer describe Yale's residential philosophy of creating a family environment where the same students live together for their entire four years.

I have written this book because I believe that every student deserves to be nurtured in the pursuit of his or her dreams and if those dreams include college, then every student needs a plan. On pages 142 and 143 of the *workbook* are worksheets to gather important information about your current middle school and the high school that you anticipate attending. You must take full advantage of the opportunities (i.e., classes, after-school programs, extracurricular activities, clubs, etc.) available at your current middle school and future high school if you are to expand your range of college choices and financial-aid opportunities.

Foreword

Students and families may question, "Is middle school too early to begin planning for college? Is that something you do during your junior year [of high school]?" It is never too late to begin developing your college plan; however, it is also never too early! In many school districts your high school plan will be greatly influenced by your elementary and middle school academic record and/or performance on standardized testing. For example, in one school district, a student must earn A's and B's in fourth and fifth grade to be placed into the AT (Academically Talented) middle school classes; in another school district, students' fourth-grade CTBS (Comprehensive Tests of Basic Skills) scores determine middle school math and science placement; and, in another school district, placement into the Talented and Gifted program is determined by students' third-grade ITBS (Iowa Tests of Basic Skills) scores.

Your sixth-grade math placement may determine the highest level of math you will be able to take in high school! As you leave middle school and enter into high school, the scope of the colleges and the majors to which you will be able to apply may have already been determined. A student interested in studying engineering in college may have had the opportunity to take Pre-Algebra (sixth grade), Algebra I (seventh grade), Geometry (eighth grade), and four years of high school math that may include Algebra II, Pre-Calculus, AP Calculus, and AP Statistics. Good grades in such classes will put a student on track to apply to a broad range of colleges and universities, whereas the student who does not enroll into advanced math until the ninth grade will have very different course selections (e.g., Algebra I, Geometry, Algebra II, and Algebra III/Trigonometry), which may not meet some colleges' admissions requirements.

As the author's younger son entered middle school he knew that he wanted to attend a local high school that offers magnet programs in math and science and in the visual and performing arts. Acceptance into the math and science magnet program requires middle school report card grades no lower than '80' in math and science during each year of middle school and that the student successfully complete Algebra I by eighth grade. Acceptance into the visual and performing arts magnet will require that he showcase and further develop his singing talent during his middle school years. His son is also utilizing his summer learning opportunities to attend academic and athletic camps. Between the sixth and seventh grades he attended the Summer Institute for the Gifted at Emory University, the NASA-sponsored Space Academy, and a football camp. After suffering a season-ending injury while playing on his middle school football team, he is already looking forward to the summer between seventh and eighth grades to return to the Summer Institute for the Gifted program and to undergo extensive training for a return to football.

Some may ask, "Why all of this fuss about college planning? I know people who did not graduate from college and they have good jobs?" In today's competitive workplace the quality of your education will enhance your ability to follow your dreams and enter into the type of career that you really want. As a young person growing up in the 21st century, you have much to encourage you. There are more jobs and career opportunities for college graduates than there are people to fill them. Every year, companies and organizations throughout the world have to recruit teachers, doctors, lawyers, nurses, policemen, business managers, hotel workers, computer technicians, and bankers. Opportunities are everywhere and you must consider yourself more than just a resident of your local community, town, city, state, or country. An education opens up the gateway to the world— to opportunities that will be yours—if you are qualified to pursue them! The opportunities for college graduates are virtually endless!

There are many books and resources that can help you to make a decision on choosing a college. There are, for example, reviews and rankings of colleges and universities by *Newsweek, U.S. News and World Reports, The Princeton Review, The Kaplan College Guide,* international publications, and Internet web sites. You also have your parents, middle school and high school counselors, and many private agencies to assist you in making your college choice based on your interests and career aspirations.

This book, and the accompanying *workbook*, provides guidance through the middle school years to assist you, the student, or parents, teachers, counselors, coaches, and mentors in developing a high school plan that will make you a strong candidate for admissions into a top college and prepared to succeed once you get there. Following the advice and strategies outlined will help to ensure that a student's dreams of attending college will not be delayed, deferred, or destroyed, as a result of not knowing how to maximize his or her opportunities by taking advantage of the wide range of programs and opportunities available during the middle school years.

As part of the plan that resulted in his acceptance into Amherst College, the author's older son played varsity football and ran the 400 Meter on his high school varsity track and field team. Not many high school track and field athletes choose to run the 400 Meter. It is a tough race that requires sprinting ability and endurance.

A successful race requires a good game plan, i.e., a strong start during the first 20 meters, sprinting while pacing yourself through the next 80 meters, breaking into a steady stride through the 200-meter mark, using your momentum to carry you around the curve through the 300-meter mark, and conserving enough energy to carry you into a full sprint during the final 100 meters.

Pursuing your dreams of attending college is going to require sprinting, steadying your pace, endurance, and a strong finish. If you are diligent at following the steps outlined in each chapter, completing the *workbook* activities, responsibly doing your schoolwork, and later, making a notable contribution to your high school and local community, you will be on your way to a successful high school experience. In addition, you will develop a strong foundation that will prepare you for college success.

Remember that part of your planning must include financing the cost of college tuition, room, and board. You and your parents must begin this aspect of college preparation as soon as possible, if you have not already done so. There are hundreds of scholarships, fellowships, grants, and low-interest loans available to assist young people in the pursuit of their college-bound dreams.

If you have a passion and/or talent in areas such as academics, sports, art, music, writing, public speaking, dance, drama, or automotive mechanics you must continue to explore every opportunity to showcase and develop your talent. Today's passion may become tomorrow's career or it may be the means of paying your way through college—the route taken by many students who have received scholarships to college because of their academic attainments, sporting abilities, creative or artistic talent, or their noteworthy contribution to their school and/or community.

There is an enormous amount of information, as well as many opportunities and support programs to pave the way for any student to attend college. In essence, there are no excuses!

Mychal Wynn
Author
Educational Consultant

Glenn Bascome, Ed.D.
Director/Dame Marjorie Bean Education Center
Sandys Secondary Middle School
Somerset, Bermuda

A Middle School Plan for Students with College-Bound Dreams

Chapter 1

Despite the constant influence of peer pressures to conform—to dress like, behave like, and follow the crowd—the uniqueness of our personalities should be as valued as the uniqueness of our signatures. Our personality represents our signature upon this life. Our personality type is unapologetically, unashamedly, and inexplicably who we are. Whether shaped divinely or through the experiences of our childhood, we must recognize who we are and accept or discard it as we continue on our journey toward becoming who we want to be.

— Mychal Wynn

Understand Who You Are

This chapter will assist you, your parents, your counselor, and perhaps your teacher or mentor to better understand you. The information that you gather in this chapter will assist you in developing your *Pre-college Profile®* (refer to *workbook*). Whether you are in elementary school, middle school, high school, or already in college, the *Pre-college Profile®* will assist you in your academic planning, personal development, and career aspirations. While race and gender are the two most obvious things we know about people, there are many more things that we can understand about ourselves and others. The activities in this chapter will assist you in learning more about:

- your personality,

- how you learn,

- how you are smart,

- how to explore your interests, and

- how to further develop your talents and abilities.

Taking the time to explore and appreciate the divinely unique person you are will help you to have a positive middle school experience. Understanding who you are can be a pretty complex and scary undertaking. For some people, after a lifetime, they still know very little about who they are, what makes them happy, and what is really important to them in life. For many students, the transition from elementary school to middle school and from middle school to high school can be difficult, disheartening, distressing, and/or disappointing. One of the major reasons for all of this confusion is that few young people, or older people for that matter, ever come to terms with who they are and how they are different from everyone else.

Each person is uniquely and divinely different. Yet, middle and high school students often focus their attention on wanting to be alike or to hide their differences. Self-consciousness, fear, and the need to be accepted cause many students to shun their differences as they spend every waking hour trying to look like, dress like, talk like, walk like, and be like everyone else. Be who you are and learn how to become the best you that you can be.

One of the first steps in understanding and appreciating your divine uniqueness is identifying your personality type. Are you the life of the party or do you enjoy quiet, meditative time? Do you prefer to focus on the facts or on people? Do you prefer to take time to gather your thoughts and create a plan of action or do you prefer to just jump right in? The answers to such questions provide insight into your unique personality.

Review the Personality Type Tables and circle each statement that best describes you when you are in public situations—those situations when you are around classmates, teammates, or at school. People oftentimes behave differently around close family and friends as opposed to when they are around other students, peers, or strangers. Since you are going to be spending a lot of time in school you should focus on the personality traits which describe how you feel about and behave in school.

Personality types

Why do we like some people or easily get along with some people while always having conflicts with others? Why do we appear to easily understand some people while being constantly confused by others? Understanding the uniqueness of our personality can help us better value and appreciate ourselves and become more understanding and accepting of others.

One of the most important factors to succeeding in school, and experiencing happiness throughout your lifetime, will be the quality of your relationships—the relationships between you and family members, between you and teachers, between you and other students, and, between you and your friends.

The relationships between ourselves and others can be better understood, and possibly strengthened, through an understanding and appreciation of personality types. As you go through each of the Personality Type Tables, you may discover that you frequently fall somewhere in the middle.

For example, you appear to be an *Extraverted* personality at times and an *Introverted* personality at other times, or you appear to be a *Feeling* personality in some situations and a *Thinking* personality in other situations. As you complete each of the Personality Type Tables, think in terms of your most common traits; few people fall totally on one side of the table or another. Most people, however, can readily identify their dominant traits. It may also be helpful to have a parent or friend complete the tables about you. Compare your results with those of your parents or friends and attempt to discover

the "real" you, which may or may not be the person whom you think that you are.

Also, keep in mind that we often demonstrate traits at school or in public that may be very different from the personality traits we demonstrate at home or with friends.

[Note: The term <u>Extravert</u> on the pages that follow is commonly referred to as <u>Extrovert</u> in contemporary literature on temperament. The term used here is <u>Extravert</u> as was originally used in the Myers-Briggs Type Indicator.]

Entering middle school can be scary but avoid believing that you have to blend in and be like everyone else. Take time to understand who you are, and better yet, to appreciate the very special person you are.

A Pledge To Myself

Today I pledge to be
  the best possible me
No matter how good I am
    I know that I can become better

Today I pledge to build
    on the work of yesterday
Which will lead me
    into the rewards of tomorrow

Today I pledge to feed
    my mind: knowledge
    my body: strength, and
    my spirit: faith

Today I pledge to reach
    new goals
    new challenges, and
    new horizons

Today I pledge to listen
    to the beat of my drummer
Who leads me onward
    in search of dreams

Today I pledge to believe in me

— Mychal Wynn

Personality Types Table I

(E) Extravert (75% of population):

1. I like variety, action, and working with others.

2. I easily meet, get to know, talk to and socialize with others.

3. I enjoy talking while working.

4. I easily communicate my thoughts and ideas in lively, even loud discussions, where people frequently interrupt others.

5. I frequently talk about things (often unrelated) as soon as they enter my mind even if I occasionally interrupt others.

6. Words that might describe me are: *Sociable, Interacting with others, Outgoing, Talkative, Lots of friends and relationships, Friendly*

(I) Introvert (25% of population):

1. I like quiet, uninterrupted time for focusing and concentrating.

2. I do not easily meet new people and sometimes have trouble remembering names and faces.

3. I prefer to think about my ideas and talk after completing my work.

4. I sometimes avoid sharing my thoughts, ideas, and opinions in large group settings unless it is agreed that everyone has an opportunity to speak.

5. If people interrupt me when I am sharing my thoughts, ideas, and opinions, I tend to stop talking and keep my thoughts to myself.

6. Words that might describe me are: *Protective of my feelings, Territorial, Inwardly Focused, Internal, Serious, Intense, Small circle of friends*

I am more of an: E   or   I   (Circle One)

Personality Types Table II

(S) Sensitive (75% of population):

1. I prefer regular assignments and consistency.

2. I prefer working through things step-by-step.

3. I prefer to know exactly what needs to be done before starting a project.

4. I am patient with routine details but I can be impatient when details become complicated.

5. I prefer an established way of doing things and I get frustrated by changes.

6. I feel good about what I already know and would prefer not to waste time experimenting with learning new ways of doing things.

7. Words that might describe me are: *Experienced, Realistic, Hard worker, Down-to-earth, Focus on the facts, Practical, Sensible*

(N) Intuitive (25% of population):

1. I like solving new problems.

2. I prefer working on a variety of things.

3. I do not like wasting time talking; just tell me what to do so that I can get started.

4. I do not like working on repetitive work and find myself driven by inspiration.

5. I am constantly thinking about how to redesign, improve, or change things.

6. I like solving new problems and continually expanding my knowledge.

7. Words that might describe me are: *Multi-tasking, Future, Focused, Speculate about the possibilities, Inspiration, Ingenious, Imaginative*

I am more of a: S   or   N   (Circle One)

Personality Types Table III

(T) Thinking (50% of population):

1. I do not usually show my feelings. I prefer dealing with facts rather than feelings.

2. I prefer to know what you think rather than how you feel.

3. I unintentionally hurt other people's feelings.

4. I like analysis, order, figuring things out and being in charge.

5. I prefer sharing my thoughts and ideas by focusing on the issues instead of on people and feelings.

6. I tend to be analytical, focusing on thoughts and ideas instead of people.

7. Words that might describe me are:
   Objective, Principles, Policy, Laws, Firm, Impersonal, Justice, Focus on the problem, Standards, Analysis

(F) Feeling (50% of population):

1. I am concerned about other people's feelings and may overlook facts to avoid hurting someone's feelings.

2. I prefer to know how people feel rather than what they think.

3. I prefer harmony and avoid discussing controversial issues to avoid conflict.

4. I do not handle personal conflicts well and may be upset long after an argument.

5. I sometimes view constructive criticism as a personal attack.

6. I am sympathetic to other people's feelings.

7. Words that might describe me are:
   Subjective, Caring, Humane, Understanding, Sympathetic, Harmonious, Appreciative

I am more of a: T   or   F   (Circle One)

Personality Types Table IV

(J) Judging (50% of population):

1. I work best when I can plan my work and follow my plan.

2. I like to reach closure. I want to complete projects, resolve issues, and move on.

3. I do not take long to make up my mind.

4. I am usually satisfied with my judgment or decision.

5. After completing a project I am ready to move on to another.

6. I do not like interruptions. Interruptions can cause me to lose my train of thought or forget some of the details.

7. Words that might describe me are: *Settled, Decided, Fixed, Plan ahead, Closure, Decision-maker, Planner, Completed, Decisive, Wrap it up, Urgent, Deadline!, Get the show on the road*

(P) Perceiving (50% of population):

1. I sometimes do not plan well.

2. I sometimes work on projects without a clear plan and find myself frequently changing my mind.

3. I sometimes leave things incomplete while I reconsider my choices.

4. I sometimes find myself having trouble making decisions; as a result, I often reopen discussions or revisit issues.

5. I occasionally jump from project to project leaving all open and incomplete.

6. I do not mind interruptions.

7. Words that might describe me are: *Pending, Gather more data, Flexible, Don't be in a hurry, Reconsider your decision, Tentative, Something will turn up, Let's wait and see, Are you sure?*

I am more of a: J   or   P   (Circle One)

Notes:

No matter how much you want to fit in and to be like everyone else, one day you will have to climb alone, you will have to discover who you are and where you are going.

My personality:

My dominant personality traits are (circle one on each line):

      (E) Extravert   *(I) Introvert*

      (S) Sensitive   *(N) Intuitive*

      (T) Thinking   *(F) Feeling*

      (J) Judging   *(P) Perceiving*

Briefly describe yourself and what you believe are your best traits, for example, outgoing, responsible, a trusted friend, a hard worker, etc.

Learning styles

Another important factor that will help you to understand who you are and to experience greater success in your middle school and high school classes is to gain an appreciation for how you learn best, or your *learning-style*. Students who learn "how they best learn" have much greater control over their success in school. While you cannot control your teacher's teaching-style, the curriculum that is being taught, how fast the curriculum is being taught, or many other dynamics in your various classrooms, you can control how you approach learning based on what you know is your unique learning-style.

Everyone has a learning-style and everyone has learning-style strengths. It is easier to learn through your strengths than it is to learn through your weaknesses. When teachers teach an entire class in exactly the same way, some students are being taught through their strengths. These students are making a connection with the teacher and appear to easily understand, process, internalize, and store the information that is being taught. These students are subsequently better able to recall the information when tests or exams are given. These students are considered to have a *teaching-style—learning-style* match. The way that the teacher teaches and the dominant way in which these students learn are in sync.

> Your *learning-style* represents the way in which you best concentrate on, process, internalize, understand, and remember new and difficult information.

At the same time some students are experiencing a *teaching-style–learning-style* match, other students are being taught through their weaknesses. These students oftentimes struggle to understand what the teacher is teaching and experience difficulty processing, internalizing, storing, and subsequently, recalling the information when taking tests and quizzes. These students have a *teaching-style–learning-style* mismatch. Most of us have experienced this *teaching-style–learning-style* mismatch.

Our older son is an example of a student who experienced a *teaching-style–learning-style* mismatch. An 'A' student in his middle school advanced math classes, however, in his tenth-grade Honors Algebra II class, he found himself experiencing difficulty understanding his teacher's teaching-style. Despite spending long hours following football practice studying, working problems, and reviewing his class notes he continued to struggle. Believing himself to understand what was being taught in class, he was baffled why he was getting failing grades on major tests. Despite having previously excelled in mathematics, he was beginning to doubt whether or not he could be successful in his math class.

His bleak outlook dramatically changed after a tutoring session with another teacher who was able to explain the material in a way that made a better connection with his learning-style. His understanding increased and his grades soared from a 30 and 50 on his pre-tutoring tests to 89 and 91 on his post-tutoring tests!

Take ownership of your learning

Most people have learning-style preferences, but individuals' preferences differ significantly. Learning-styles reflects an individuals' personal reactions to each of 21 elements *when concentrating on new and difficult academic knowledge or skills.* To capitalize on your learning-styles, you need to be aware of your:

21 Learning-style Elements:

Environmental:

1. *Sound*
2. *Light*
3. *Temperature*
4. *Design*

Emotional:

5. *Motivation*
6. *Persistence*
7. *Responsibility*
8. *Structure*

Sociological:

9. *Self*
10. *Pair*
11. *Peers*
12. *Team*
13. *Adult*
14. *Varied*

Physical:

15. *Perceptual*
16. *Intake*
17. *Time*
18. *Mobility*

Psychological:

19. *Global/Analytic*
20. *Hemisphericity*
21. *Impulsive/Reflective*

- reactions to the immediate classroom environment—background noise such as music and talking versus silence, bright light versus soft lighting, warm versus cool temperatures, and formal (i.e., desk and chair) versus informal (i.e., bed, floor, or bean bag) seating;

- emotional state—motivated, persistent, responsible, and able to exercise control over the learning environment versus a classroom setting that is largely controlled by the teacher with teacher-imposed deadlines, rules, etc.;

- social preferences—working alone, with friends or classmates, with an adult, and/or in a variety of ways as opposed to teacher-determined patterns or routines;

- physiological preferences—perceptual strengths (auditory, visual, tactual, and/or kinesthetic strengths), time-of-day energy levels, intake (snacking while concentrating), and/or mobility needs.

The belief that there is one best way for students to learn is a widely-held misconception. Many teachers attribute student failure to lack of motivation, lack of interest, poor study habits, or simply lack of the intellectual capacity to succeed in certain subject areas. However, the reality is that people remember new and difficult information through different perceptual modalities. For those of you who are asking, "Perceptual what?" it means that people learn differently. Parents of children who learn visually are oftentimes guilty of saying, "In one ear—out the other." They wonder why their children are not successful remembering or following verbal instructions. Such students may simply be visual learners. They do not learn best and struggle to successfully follow instructions when they are "told" the steps. They need to "see" the steps.

The typical middle school classroom will represent a wide variety of learning styles.  Although most teachers spend a good deal of time teaching by talking, learning-by-listening is usually the most difficult way for most people to remember new and challenging information. On average, 30 percent or more of students are unable to remember at least 75 percent of what they either hear or see. They are neither strongly auditory (learn by hearing) nor visual (learn by seeing) learners. Some, particularly elementary and middle school students, remember well when they learn tactually (with their hands) and/or kinesthetically or experientially (with their bodies—through movement). As your personality type reflects who you uniquely are, your learning style reflects how you uniquely learn.

- Some people learn best by reading.

- Some learn best from cartoons, graphs, pictures, photographs, diagrams, or transparencies than they do from printed words or numbers.

- Combinations of listening and reading are effective for people who learn well from films, movies, or videotapes. On the other hand, some people find multimedia teaching distracting and find it difficult to focus on more than one stimulus (sight and sound) at a time.

Time-of-day energy levels

Did you know that time-of-day energy levels can also impact on your ability to learn? Are you most alert in the morning or evening? Or, do you learn and/or perform best during the late morning or afternoon? You will have to work a lot harder to be successful at your wrong time of day. If you are an early-morning learner, you will benefit by scheduling your most difficult classes in the morning when you are most focused. If you do not have any control over your class schedule you may benefit from eating high-energy snacks during your low-energy time-of-day.

Some students learn best by interacting with their teachers, but others prefer learning independently. This preference is also reflective of a student's personality type. Introverted personalities prefer to work independently. They appear to focus and concentrate better without the distraction of being around other people. Some students enjoy learning with a friend, sometimes in a group and some like a little of everything—alone, with a friend, in a group and with their teacher or coach. While many students have been successful at adapting their primary learning style to their schools and teachers, other students oftentimes find themselves struggling. They discover that they have only one favorite way of learning and experience a great deal of difficulty adapting or learning in any other way.

Everyone has strengths. Mothers and fathers often learn differently from each other and from their children. Nevertheless, parents commonly insist that children study and do their homework as they themselves did when they were young. That approach is not likely to be effective for at least some of the children because within the same family different individuals usually learn in diametrically opposite ways.

The terms analytic/global, left/right, sequential/ simultaneous, and inductive/deductive are used interchangeably to describe some of the many different ways people learn. What is crucial to understand is that you are capable of becoming a successful learner if you are taught through instructional methods or resources that complement your learning style.

You will learn, remember better, and enjoy learning more when you are taught, or study, through your learning-style preferences. At this stage of your life you are going to find that you have little control over how your teachers teach or the textbooks that are assigned. However, what you can control is better understanding how you best learn and finding ways to supplement your teacher's teaching style and course materials with your dominant learning style and supplemental materials. Any mismatch, while hindering you from learning, does not mean

that you are incapable, unable, or uninterested. Your success in school and in life is greatly enhanced if you can learn how you learn and learn how to re-learn information that is taught in ways that are confusing in the classroom.

Do you need a tutor?

My wife and I have learned that to ensure the success of our children, we must identify tutors who can make a better connection with their learning styles whenever they find themselves struggling with their classroom teachers. Tutors, while once thought of as being needed by students who are slow to learn, can be a necessity for students who are not making a connection with their classroom teachers or who are simply having difficulty comprehending or understanding new concepts. As you will soon learn, there are at least eight ways of being smart and no two individuals are smart in exactly the same way. It follows that there are at least eight ways of being  weak. One person may effortlessly understand complicated mathematical processes and equations while another will need a tutor. One person may effortlessly compose poetry, write short stories, or write research papers while another will find himself or herself in need of help. Keep in mind that when you submit your college application and transcript, the admissions officer is not going to care about any mismatch between your learning style and your teachers' teaching styles. He or she is only going to be concerned with your grades! If you need help, do not be embarrassed to ask for it.

As previously stated, there are many types of learning styles, i.e., global, analytic, auditory, kinesthetic, tactile, visual, verbal, sensing, intuitive, etc. Your counselor may be able to provide a learning-style assessment or you can go to the Internet and do a keyword search on "learning styles assessments" for a listing of web sites. Another approach is to keep a learning-styles journal where you record how you study, your best/worst learning situations, and the type of environment in which you prefer to study (e.g., quiet, noisy, background music, talking, eating, bright lights, relaxing, formal, etc.). Over time you will gain a better understanding of the situations in which you best learn.

Identify your best learning situations

1. Identify the subjects or classes where you appeared to learn the most or did the best and write down as much as you can remember about such things as how the teacher taught, the type of classroom environment, how students related to each other or worked together, the type and amount of class work and/or homework, how interesting the subject was, whether or not the teacher told stories or made jokes, and what was fun, challenging, or interesting about the entire classroom experience.

2. Identify the subjects or classes where you received low grades or had difficulty learning. Write down the types of things that caused you difficulty or that you struggled with.

3. Think about the tests on which you have done really well. Reflect on how you studied, how long you studied, what you did to help you to remember the information that was going to be covered on the test, or if the teacher provided a study guide and/or supplemental materials.

4. Think about the tests where you performed poorly. Reflect on what caused you difficulty and/or whether or not you prepared for the test in the same way as you did for those tests on which you performed well.

5. Think about when you learn best or do your best work. Reflect on the time of day, whether or not you work with others or work alone, whether or not you are under a time schedule or if you work at your own pace, whether or not the environment is quiet or if there is music, talking, or background noise.

Three students, in the same classroom and with the same books are likely to have different learning styles.

6. Think about the classes or subjects for which you can still remember a lot of what was taught. What was unique about those classes or subjects? Reflect on whether you worked with your hands, created songs, performed experiments, prepared skits, took field trips, listened to guest speakers, received pre-printed notes from the teacher or created your own notes, etc.

7. Make a list of the subjects or activities that you are most interested in and reflect on why you like these subjects or have these areas of interest.

8. Make a list of the subjects or activities that you like the least and reflect on why you do not have an interest in these subjects or activities.

9. If you could design the ideal classroom experience for yourself, what would it be?

10. If you could design the ideal study location at home, where would it be?

11. What is the ideal time of day for your most difficult classes?

How you are smart

Dr. Howard Gardner, in his research on Multiple Intelligences, shows that each of us has, or can demonstrate intelligence in at least eight ways and there may be many more. Sometimes when a person is really good at a sport like basketball, we may consider him or her as being talented but we are unlikely to view his or her basketball playing ability as being smart. "You got game!" not, "You got brains!" However, when a person masterfully dribbles a basketball or soccer ball, he or she is actually demonstrating highly developed *Bodily/Kinesthetic Intelligence*. This is the part of the human brain that controls body movement and hand-eye coordination.

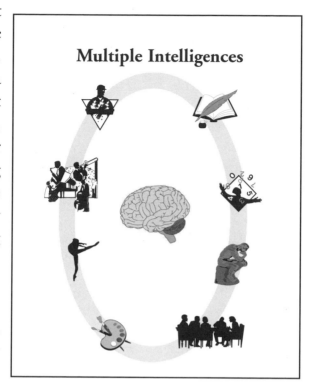

Multiple Intelligences

Verbal/Linguistic

Logical/Mathematical

Intrapersonal

Interpersonal

Visual/Spatial

Bodily/Kinesthetic

Musical/Rhythmic

Naturalist

The person who expertly illustrates comic book characters, cartoons, or puts together color-coordinated stylish outfits has highly developed *Visual/Spatial Intelligence*, not just an eye for fashions or drawing talent. The person who has a highly developed intuition in understanding animals and animal behaviors, camping, hiking, or surviving in the natural environment is highly developed in what is called the *Naturalist Intelligence*. There are many ways to demonstrate intelligence and many types of intelligences. No matter how much you may excel in one subject or struggle in another, you are likely to experience both highly developed and weak areas of intelligence. In some subjects you are likely to appear a genius and in other subjects not very smart at all.

Read the summary
for each of the
eight intelligences
and reflect on those
intelligences where
you best learn or
most easily apply
what you know.

For example, some
people effortlessly
write poetry while
struggling with
math, others struggle
with sharing their
thoughts verbally
while easily
illustrating cartoons
or designing things.

Each student will
experience strong
areas and weak
areas, however, no
one area is more
important than
another.

Review the Multiple
Intelligences Tables
that follow and
place a check next to
each statement that
describes you. Tally
your checks for each
intelligence and
place your total for
each intelligence in
the box next to the
intelligence.

Verbal/Linguistic

I am good at things like reading, writing, talking, and debating.

I like things like poetry, humor, storytelling, debating, and creative writing.

Logical/Mathematical

I am good at figuring things out, analyzing things, and solving problems in subjects like math and science.

I like things like figuring out patterns, matching things that are alike, math, science, crossword puzzles, and solving problems.

Intrapersonal

I am good at self-reflection and being in touch with my feelings. I am also good at focusing, concentrating, and thinking things through.

*I like things like closing my eyes and reflecting about how I feel about things, focusing, concentrating, and engaging in inner reflection.
I like meditating and thinking about things and I often prefer working alone or in small groups.*

Interpersonal

I am good at working with other people and working on group projects. I am also good at sharing my opinion with other people and understanding their opinions and how they feel about things.

I like working with other people on group projects and being a member of a team.

Visual/Spatial

I am good at creating pictures in my mind and drawing them. I am also good at creative and artistic things like using colors or reading maps, and I have a good imagination.

I like to draw, paint, create sculptures, and imagine things.

Bodily/Kinesthetic

I am good at things like sports, dance, gymnastics, martial arts, and boxing. I am also good at working with my hands. I have good body control and coordination.

I like things like playing sports, dancing, exercising, swimming, skating, riding bicycles, running, and building things.

Musical/Rhythmic

I like singing, playing musical instruments, beating drums, humming, writing songs, and performing.

I am good at things like picking up sounds and tones, keeping a beat and remembering melodies.

Naturalist

I enjoy working and being outdoors, watching birds, insects, and animals. I like outdoor activities like hiking, camping, fishing, or exploring.

I am good at working outdoors with plants or animals. I have a heightened sense of understanding of plants, animals, or changes in weather patterns.

Verbal/Linguistic ☐

_____ I enjoy reading

_____ I enjoy telling stories

_____ I enjoy creating stories, poetry, or raps

_____ I am good at writing about my thoughts or ideas

_____ I am good at talking about my thoughts or ideas

_____ I have a good understanding of things when there are written instructions

_____ I enjoy reading about my hobbies or interests (e.g, books, news articles, magazines)

_____ I remember things best when I have a list or by reading about them

_____ I enjoy word games like Scrabble or word puzzles

_____ When working in groups or on teams I enjoy doing the research or writing the presentation

Logical/Mathematical ☐

_____ I am good at problem-solving in subjects like math and science

_____ I enjoy doing experiments or figuring out complex problems

_____ I enjoy asking questions and figuring out how things work

_____ I believe that I have a logical mind and I am good at critical thinking

_____ I am good at developing plans

_____ I am good at organizing things into a step-by-step fashion

_____ I am good at gathering data or analyzing information

_____ I enjoy sharing my thoughts and ideas

_____ I enjoy math, problem-solving, or strategy games

_____ When working in groups or on teams I enjoy creating charts/graphs or organizing the presentation

Interpersonal ☐

_____ I get along well with others

_____ I have good friendships

_____ I enjoy talking to or communicating with others

_____ I am good at understanding others

_____ I feel comfortable at parties and large gatherings of people

_____ I am good at organizing teams

_____ I am good at building relationships

_____ I am good at cooperating or collaborating with others

_____ I empathize with others and their feelings

_____ When working in groups or on teams I enjoy working with my team members and prefer to reach a consensus on important decisions

Intrapersonal ☐

_____ I am inwardly focused and self-directed

_____ I am good at being in touch with my feelings

_____ I enjoy concentrating on my thoughts

_____ I do not mind working alone

_____ I enjoy meditating and daydreaming

_____ I prefer self-directed projects

_____ I prefer to have my own space and move at my own pace

_____ I prefer to gather my thoughts before participating in group discussions

_____ I tend to have a small group of friends whom I am really close to

_____ When working in groups or on teams I enjoy accepting tasks that I can work on independently

Visual/Spatial ▢

_____ I am good at creating pictures in my mind

_____ I am good at drawing

_____ I enjoy creating models or designing things

_____ I have a good imagination

_____ I am good at choosing clothing or hair styles

_____ I prefer to see a picture or a diagram of how something works

_____ I am good at directions or reading maps

_____ I enjoy interior design

_____ I have a lot of creative ideas

_____ When working in groups or on teams I do not mind being responsible for creating the cover and/or design or layout the presentation

Bodily/Kinesthetic ▢

_____ I am good at sports

_____ I enjoy dancing

_____ I am good at building things or working with my hands

_____ I am good at creating new gymnastics, martial arts, or boxing movements

_____ I am good at roller skating

_____ I enjoy riding bicycles, skiing, or snowboarding

_____ I have good body coordination

_____ I find it easy to learn new sports or dance moves

_____ I enjoy putting things together and repairing things

_____ When working in groups or on teams I enjoy presenting a demonstration through dance, gymnastics, or other ways in which I can use my body

Musical/Rhythmic ▢

_____ I enjoy singing

_____ I enjoy playing an instrument

_____ I easily remember tunes, songs, or lyrics

_____ I am good at keeping a beat or remembering a melody

_____ I enjoy writing songs or creating musical compositions

_____ I am good at picking up sounds

_____ I tend to hum or tap a beat when I am working or thinking

_____ I am good at mixing music

_____ I like music playing while I study

_____ When working in groups or on teams I enjoy creating theme songs or selecting background music

Naturalist ▢

_____ I am good at hiking, camping, fishing, and living in the environment

_____ I am good at understanding and working with animals

_____ I enjoy working or being outdoors

_____ I would enjoy survivalist competitions

_____ I have a good feeling of what is going on around me

_____ I would enjoy living or working on a farm

_____ I am good at identifying insects or tracking animals

_____ I notice cloud and rock formations

_____ I can feel changes in weather patterns

_____ When working in groups or on teams I enjoy creating the stage arrangements or building a backdrop

The information that you gather will help you to better understand how you are smart. People who are good in music, art, or sports have always been called "gifted" or "talented," but not necessarily "smart." Athletes have always been called "jocks" (sometimes jokingly referred to as "dumb jocks"). Their athletic abilities were identified simply as representing athletic prowess, gifts, or natural abilities. Now we know that their abilities, as demonstrated in their respective sport, represent the highest form of *Bodily/Kinesthetic Intelligence*.

While the *Bodily/Kinesthetic Intelligence* of the athlete may be his or her most dominant intelligence, it is not the only intelligence that he or she has developed or can develop. Becoming involved in a variety of activities or clubs such as the chess club, math club, science club, chorus, band, student government, or hiking can assist in developing a wide range of intelligences leading to a broad range of hobbies or career opportunities.

David Robinson, former professional basketball player, Olympic Goal Medalist, and NBA Most Valuable Player for the San Antonio Spurs, played classical piano, scored highly on the SAT, graduated with honors from the United States Naval Academy, and is recognized as a computer genius. His intelligences have been developed far beyond the Bodily/Kinesthetic Intelligence demonstrated through his skills on the basketball court.

[Ten Steps to Helping Your Child Succeed in School]

What are your dreams?

The more that you learn about yourself, the more you can appreciate the divinely unique person you are and the unique dreams and aspirations you may develop. Take a moment to reflect on what you have learned and ask yourself, "If I could spend four years in college studying what I have a passion for, what would I study?" And, "If I could do what I love to do and get paid to do it, what type of job would I have?" Rather than trying to emulate or imitate someone else, understand who you are, appreciate your uniqueness, and become the best you!

Strengths and weaknesses

This chapter has assisted you in better understanding who you are, how you learn, and how you are smart.

After reflecting on what you have learned, identify your strengths and weaknesses as they pertain to your school and school work. Preparing for college will require that you succeed in middle school now and high school later. Middle school is the time in the lives of many young people when they begin to pull away from their parents. There are likely to be many disagreements on the horizon as your parents place a priority on school and school work and you begin to place your priorities on friends and after-school activities.

As previously mentioned, middle school is going to be more difficult than elementary school. You are going to get more homework, take more tests and quizzes, and have far more responsibilities. Identifying your strengths and weaknesses will help you and your parents to identify where you are likely to encounter challenges. My wife and I have helped both of our sons identify their respective strengths and weaknesses, which has led to both their academic success and social development.

When our older son was attending middle school, to compensate for his lack of organization, we began keeping a monthly calendar of all of his homework, quiz, tests, and project due dates. We also added his after-school and weekend activities. We posted a copy of his calendar onto the wall in his bedroom and a copy onto the refrigerator. He learned to accept that we, as his parents, had more organizational skills than he had and that we were better able to help him to stay aware of important dates and to set aside the necessary time to prepare for tests and quizzes. He accepted that his responsibility was to note homework, quiz and test dates, and project due dates in his planner as soon as they were announced in class. We accepted the responsibility of transferring the information in his planner to the master calendar at home.

The daily routine that we have developed for our younger son, who is currently in the seventh grade, takes into account his strengths (being well organized) and his weaknesses (forgetting what his daily responsibilities are).

Whatever your strengths and weaknesses, you have to be honest with yourself and identify them. We have sat around the dinner table and helped both of our sons to identify their respective strengths and weaknesses in the areas of class work, homework, tests, and completing projects. It took a while, but the more that they were able to accept their weaknesses without getting upset or feeling that my wife and I were unfairly criticizing them, the more they were able to identify strategies to overcome, or compensate for, their respective weaknesses and expand upon their respective strengths.

Take time to identify your strengths and weaknesses in such areas as class work, homework, organization, note-taking, test preparation, reading, writing, and within your various subjects, i.e., math, science, social studies, foreign language, etc. Talk to your parents, teacher, counselor, or coach about ways to overcome your weaknesses and to further develop and expand upon your strengths. Review what you have learned in this chapter and refer to the *workbook* and complete the *Pre-college Profile® Part I.*

Chapter 2

As competition grows tougher at all the top colleges, the game of getting into these schools has become more and more complex. No matter who you are or how good your grades and test scores are, there is no guarantee that you will be admitted to your desired schools. You must commit yourself to putting in a valiant effort if you want to compete in this game where students and college counselors are increasingly using sophisticated timing, marketing, and information-relaying strategies in order to get ahead.

In order to be confident that you will do your best in the process, you must research your college and program options, finding those that best fit your needs and desires; understand college admissions, recognizing application options such as Early Decision and identifying the goals or philosophies of the admissions officers at your target schools; and then, based on information gained during these first two tasks, launch a sophisticated application and marketing strategy.

— [How to Get into the Top Colleges]

Why College?

The four years of college for the young person just graduating from high school will provide a once-in-a-lifetime opportunity to grow socially, emotionally, and intellectually. The college experience provides an opportunity for exposure to people, information, ideas, debates, and discussions that can shape a young person's life for adulthood, marriage, and parenthood. The earning potential and career opportunities for college graduates can lead a young person into the pursuit of dreams that, as a middle school student, may be unimaginable. However, attending

and graduating from college is not simply about getting a better job, entering into a more prestigious career, or earning the right to say that you attended a top-ranked university; it is about the opportunity to learn, to grow, to give back to your university, to make a contribution to your community, and to provide a legacy from which others will be inspired. Your college degree automatically provides substantially greater earning potential

and career options than a high school diploma; graduating from a top-ranked university provides you with admittance into a brother/sisterhood of thousands of alumni who are influential in education, politics, business, government, and organizations throughout the United States and the world.

Students and parents reading this book are likely to have differing ideas and opinions about the value of college planning before high school, let alone pursuing a college

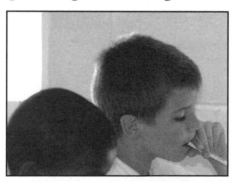

education after high school. For some families, there is no doubt that their children will attend college. For other families, there is much doubt and many roadblocks such as the belief that their children do not possess the academic ability, that their children will not be accepted into college, that there will not be enough money to pay for college, or that college is not necessary. Following is the short list of comments that I have heard from students, teachers, and parents:

Parent to child: "I don't care what you say, you are going to college—period!"

Child to parent: "I don't want to go to college, I've been in school long enough. I'm looking forward to hanging out with my friends."

Parent to another parent: "You know, my son struggled all the way through school. I just don't think that he is smart enough to go to college."

Teacher to another teacher: "These kids don't need to think about going to college. College isn't for everyone, you know."

Parent to another parent: "My daughter is talking about going to college but I don't have enough money to pay for college."

Student to another student: "I'm going to apply to as many colleges as I can, someone is going to let me in."

Student to another student: "I don't need to think about college until I get to high school—maybe, not even until I graduate."

Basketball player: "I am going to college on an athletic scholarship, I don't need to pay attention to school work, the coach will get someone to do the work for me."

Student who is daydreaming: "I want to make a million trillion dollars. Can they teach me how to do that in college?"

Student to his mother: "Mama, did you go to college?"

While some students have parents or other relatives who have graduated from college and have people outside of school whom they can rely on to assist them in developing their plan, other students do not have any family members who have graduated from college and may not have the confidence that they can be the first in their family to earn a college degree.

No matter which student you are, do not allow anyone to discourage you from pursuing your dreams or to convince you that you are not "college material." It is impossible to grasp the full range of options and opportunities that a college education will provide. During the college experience itself you will explore career options and opportunities never previously considered. Your degree will provide you with an opportunity to choose from hundreds of career opportunities from financial management to fashion design, education to entrepreneurship, architecture to archeology, medical technology to marine biology, politics to philosophy, internal medicine to international business, or ambassador to anesthesiologist. A college degree will provide unparalleled opportunity to change career paths, pursue new interests, acquire new jobs, and explore new industries long after graduation. In a word, a college degree is a 'key' that can unlock hundreds of doors and opportunities throughout your entire adult life.

How is your college literacy?

- What is the difference between an AA and a BA degree?

- What two college admissions exams are accepted for admission into most U.S. colleges and what is the top score on each exam?

- What does Alma mater mean?

- What does Legacy student mean?

- What does FAFSA mean?

- What does Base Year mean?

- What does COA mean?

- What is Need-Based–Need-Blind Admissions?

- What does FAO mean?

- What does your Award Letter outline?

- What does HBCU mean?

- How many colleges make up the Ivy League?

- What students must register with the NCAA Clearinghouse?

- Who is the Valedictorian?

- Who is the Salutatorian?

- What is a viewbook?

- What are the SAT IIs and when should they be taken?

- What is joint enrollment?

Not only are these some of the many questions and college admissions terminology that you should know the answers to but you will need to know the high school graduation requirements and the admissions requirements for your top-choice colleges.

What do you know about college?

Some students have had a great deal of exposure to colleges and universities through their parents, older siblings, and college visits. However, no matter how much exposure you may or may not have had to an actual college campus, you can learn a lot about various colleges from teachers, counselors, principals, church members, family, and family friends who have attended college.

Careers

While the four-year college experience can be a once-in-a-lifetime opportunity in itself, college is an important step toward a variety of careers. While your knowledge of the multitude of career opportunities is often limited to the careers of teachers, family members, and jobs available within your local community, there are many more careers that college will expose you to and prepare you for. For example, have you ever considered a career as an Anthropologist; Cytotechnologist; Actuary; Novelist; or Sommelier? A college education will provide you with hundreds of career options and opportunities.

In addition to the many unrelated careers that college will expose you to, there are many related careers that you may pursue simultaneously while attending college. For example, while playing a college sport in the pursuit of a career as a professional athlete you may also pursue a career as a sports agent or athletic trainer through your college studies.

Early College

One of the initial activities that you and your parents could engage in would be to research Early College programs. Such programs are available to students as early as elementary school and offer the opportunity for students to take college-level classes as early as middle school. TIP (Talent Identification Program) at Duke University and the Center for Talented Youth program at Johns Hopkins University are two such programs.

Overall, the purpose for answering the question, "Why college?" at this early stage, is to assist you and your parents in focusing your efforts over the course of your middle-through-high school years. There will be many things to do so that you prepare yourself for the type of college that you will ultimately apply for admissions to and there will be many opportunities for you to increase your chances of being accepted into the colleges that you apply to.

The activities in *Section II: Why College?*, of the *workbook,* will further direct you toward researching colleges and the importance of initiating contact with the colleges that you are interested in while you are attending middle school.

Chapter 3

The middle school years provide an extraordinary opportunity for young people to discover themselves, their hopes, their dreams, and their destination in life. It is an unparalleled opportunity to lay the foundation that will allow them to enjoy their high school experience.

— Mychal Wynn

Elementary—Middle School Transition

Most students are both excited and apprehensive about the transition from elementary to middle school. Will I see my old friends? Will I make new friends? Will I like my teachers? Who will I sit with in the cafeteria? Will I have any conflicts with anyone? The successful transition from elementary to middle school will require that you utilize your elementary school experience as a foundation to build upon. Use the skills that you developed in elementary school to avoid conflicts and to stay focused on your daily responsibilities and school work for a successful middle school transition.

Taking the time to reflect on where you excelled and where you may have faced challenges in elementary school can help prepare you for what is ahead in middle school. All of the subjects taken during elementary school will also be required in middle and high school. Make a plan for coping with subjects you do not like and/or have difficulty with. Make a plan with your parents to participate in your favorite activities outside of school. You will have many positive experiences during your middle school years, however, you will also encounter conflicts. How you handle these conflicts will impact upon how well you adjust to your middle school experience. If you or your parents need help with your plans, please do not hesitate to ask your school counselor for assistance.

Notes:

Who are your friends?

At the beginning of each school year, students are confronted with many types of social decisions from what to wear to what clubs or school activities to become involved in. Perhaps the most difficult decision you will make will involve choosing your friends. Some students have friends from their schools and community. Other students, new to a school or community, are forced to make choices of which groups to identify with, the types of people to socialize with, and subsequently who to become friends with.

Become a leader

Oftentimes we are influenced by others to do things that we otherwise would not do. Many students violate school policy or become involved in fighting or bullying as a result of the peer pressure of friends or classmates. Peer pressure is not limited to young people but is common in every society with people of every age. Preschool children become part of groups that break toys, elementary school children become part of groups that call other children names, middle school students become part of groups that bully other students, and the examples continue on to adults who become part of groups who commit criminal acts. You must carefully choose who you follow and become a leader for others to follow.

What is your mission?

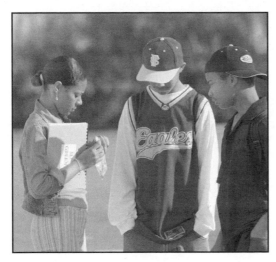

As the school year begins, you will be confronted with many decisions and you will receive conflicting advice from friends, classmates, teachers, counselors, your parents, and other family members.

Beginning the school year with a mission, or a purpose, can make all of the difference between a great school year or a miserable one, and between achieving goals or wandering aimlessly without purpose or direction. While the strategies and activities contained within this book will place you on course to pursue your college-bound dreams, they will be of little use unless you have a personal mission to succeed.

Prepare for school success

Before you can begin preparing for college or career opportunities tomorrow you must prepare yourself to succeed in middle school today. Preparing for school success requires that you do some work in and outside of school. Speak with your counselor about developing a résumé and career portfolio. At home you can establish a place to store all of your current school information as well as all of the college and financial-aid information gathered over the next several years. Although college for a sixth-grade student is seven years away, before you know it you will be sitting down completing college applications, filling out financial-aid forms, and putting together your college admissions packages.

The information that you begin gathering now will become a part of your college application package which you will complete and/or submit during your senior year of high school. Depending on the type of college and/or college program that you apply to, you may be required to submit some or all of the following forms and information:

- admissions application and financial-aid forms
- admissions and financial-aid essays
- high school transcript
- SAT/ACT scores
- academic profile
- personal profile
- résumé
- athletic profile (if you are planning to compete as a college athlete)
- extracurricular, employment, and community service information
- portfolio (if you are an artist, photographer, etc.)
- recommendation letters

The college and scholarship information that you will be researching will not only be important to assisting you in the pursuit of your dreams, but will be valuable to share with relatives, friends, and classmates who are also planning on attending college.

Many families learn that by working with other families to gather the plethora (plethora is one of your SAT words ... more about that later) of financial aid and college information that they are able to accomplish much more than by working alone. Consider developing *College Planning* and *Financial-Aid Planning* teams with each group of parents or students concentrating on one area of research and gathering information on college admissions requirements, scholarship opportunities, community service program opportunities, summer programs, SAT/ACT preparation courses, etc.

Understand teacher expectations

Understand the grading scale and pay attention to the course syllabus outlining how grades for each of your classes will be computed. A course syllabus usually outlines grades in such areas as:

- Homework
- Quizzes
- Tests
- Mid-term/Final Exams
- Class work
- Class Participation
- Projects
- Extra Credit

Develop a plan of how you are going to get the highest possible grade in each of your classes:

- Do not miss "free" points. If your teacher offers extra credit, these are free points.

- Do not miss the "easy" points. Participate in classroom discussions, do the homework, and turn the homework in on time.

- Identify your weaknesses. If you do not do well on tests, talk to your teacher about ways of better preparing for tests and quizzes. If there is not a good connection between your learning style and the teacher's teaching style, talk to your teacher or a tutor about what you can do to compensate.

Take advantage of the classroom discussions during homeroom/advisory and counselor lessons pertaining to

organization, test preparation, and study skills. The study habits, test preparation, and organizational skills that you develop, or fail to develop, in middle school will either help or hurt you in high school. Developing the proper study and note-taking skills will provide the foundation for a good start in high school and will put you on track for the most challenging classes and on course toward the highest academic achievement.

Get involved in activities

Some clubs and activities will allow you to continue to pursue your interests while other activities will allow you to explore new interests. Taking the time to reflect on where you excelled and where you may have faced challenges in elementary school can help to prepare you for what is ahead in middle school. Your counselor or advisor can assist in identifying the middle school programs that will provide further opportunity to explore your interests as well as help you to identify supplemental materials and/or additional assistance that you may need for those subjects or areas in which you experienced difficulty.

Deal with disagreements

Disagreements are inevitable. They may result from someone sitting in your seat on the school bus, bumping into you in the cafeteria, or having a different point of view during a classroom discussion. Discipline infractions can disqualify you from participating in clubs, activities, and after-school programs. In some school districts, discipline infractions during middle school will disqualify students from applying to some high schools and/or high school programs. Ultimately, how you handle disagreements can have a direct impact on where you go to college or whether or not you are even able to go to college.

Ten steps to preparing for academic success

Many students experience difficulty in the elementary to middle school transition. Students find themselves falling behind academically by the time that the first progress reports are issued and continue to struggle with organization, turning in assignments on time, and effectively preparing for tests and quizzes. Students who are involved in a sport such as football or activity such as cheerleading may also find themselves falling behind in their school work.

The following steps can assist you in making a smooth transition into middle school and well on the way to experiencing academic success and a successful sixth-grade school year.

Step 1: Get organized

Middle schools have more students and teachers than elementary school and you will be expected to become more independent and personally responsible. As opposed to one elementary school classroom teacher, as a middle school student you may have a different teacher for each subject. As opposed to a single desk in a single classroom, you are likely to

sit in different desks, in different locations, with different students and/or teachers every 40-90 minutes throughout the school day. You must quickly learn to remember class schedules, classroom locations, classroom procedures, and homework assignments in six to eight different classes.

Amidst all of this is the fact that, as a fifth-grade student, you may have found yourself among the biggest and most mature students in your elementary school. However, as a sixth-grade student, you may find yourself among the smallest and least mature students in your middle school. Dealing effectively with all of this and staying on track academically will require proper planning and preparation.

Get into the habit of keeping your work organized. Your teachers will tell you the materials that you need for their class. Place an accordion folder or pocket folders in your backpack to keep your papers until you have the opportunity to place them into the appropriate subject-binder—no crumpled papers!

After receiving a class schedule and/or course syllabus:

- Meet with each of your teachers and ask for their advice on how to set up a binder, notebook, or folder in a way which will assist you in being best prepared for their class.

- Make copies of your class schedule and post one in your school locker, one onto your refrigerator at home, one into the glove compartment of your family car, and one into your student planner.

- Place the course syllabus for each class into the front of the appropriate binder. Do not place it into the pocket in the binder, IT WILL GET LOST!

- Create an assignment log and note all of your assignments onto your assignment log. (Note: some students do not find it necessary to maintain an assignment log, they use their student planner to track their grades and assignments.)

- Develop a daily routine of punching holes into all of your important papers and placing them into the rings, behind the appropriate tab, of the appropriate subject-binder.

- Note the due date of the assignment and the date that you turn in each assignment onto your assignment log.

- Immediately after graded assignments are returned, place them behind the appropriate tab (i.e., quiz, test, homework, etc.) and note the grade onto your assignment log.

- Organize yourself in the way which enables you to best track your assignments and grades.

Middle school teachers have so many students and grade so many papers that you may experience an occasion where a teacher misplaces your assignment or fails to note your grade into his or her grade book. Keeping track of what you turn in and the grades that you receive can mean the difference between earning a grade, receiving a zero, or having to redo the assignment.

Keep your student planner up-to-date. Immediately mark test, quiz, and homework dates as they are announced. If your teacher writes the day's homework assignment onto the board or announces it in class, take the time to write it down in your planner as soon as you get to class or as soon as the teacher announces it.

Step 2: Develop daily routines

Middle school success like successful athletic competition requires creating a training schedule and pre-competition plan. An athlete competing in basketball, track and field, football, baseball, rugby, or gymnastics does not just show up at the meet, match, or game and expect to win. He or she trains physically and mentally by developing a nutritional plan, training schedule, and engaging in pre-game mental preparation. After receiving your class schedule, you have to take a moment and reflect on your life, the activities that you are involved in, and the amount of time that you have each day to:

- prepare for school,
- travel to school,
- organize your homework and class work,
- travel home from school,
- participate in any after-school activities,
- complete your homework, and
- study.

Together with your parents, answer the following questions. Develop the routine which best meets your needs and personality.

1. How much time will you need in the morning to get organized for school?

2. How much time will you need to prepare and eat breakfast?

3. Will you take your lunch to school and if so, how much time will you need to prepare it?

4. Where will you put your binders, books, and/or backpack in the evening?

5. When will you punch holes in your papers and organize them in the appropriate subject-binder?

6. When will you do your homework?

7. What nights do you have extracurricular activities that may interfere with your homework routine?

8. What days will you go to school early or stay late to meet with teachers or for tutoring?

9. What time do you need to get to bed and how much sleep do you need to be at your best?

10. When will you iron, wash, or lay out your school clothes?

While some questions may appear silly, thoughtfully answering them will assist you and your family in developing an effective before- and after-school routine that will most certainly help you and your family to avoid unnecessary stress and frustration. After reflecting on your answers, complete the daily routine worksheet in the *workbook*.

Try your routine for a week and make adjustments as needed to put yourself on the best possible schedule. Post your routine in a convenient location as a daily reminder. Do your best to follow your routine as closely as possible and check off each item as you meet your target time so that you can see how much you are able to remain on track. Remember, this is your plan and this is your future.

Step 3: Develop consistent classroom routines

As you consciously organize your before- and after-school routines, you must also develop consistent classroom routines.

For example:

1. Enter the classroom and take out your planner and subject-binder.

2. Make note of the day's homework and/or quiz/test date in your planner.

3. Remove the current homework or previous day's class work from your subject-binder.

4. Place any handouts, notes, or returned assignments into your subject-binder or accordion folder.

5. Place class notes behind the appropriate tab.

While such a routine may be considered an inconvenience initially, over the course of an entire school year it will become a simplistic and consistent method of keeping your assignments organized and ensuring that you are aware of announced tests and quizzes.

Step 4: Learn how to take good notes

Taking effective notes is critical to your middle school academic success. Hopefully, you learned how to take good notes in elementary school; however, if you have not developed good note-taking skills, you must bring this to the attention of your teacher, advisor, or counselor. They will be able to make suggestions to prevent you from getting off to a rocky start in middle school.

There is no one-size-fits-all for effective note-taking. The purpose of note-taking is to record important information that is being taught by your teacher so that you may later review and prepare for tests and quizzes. Each student must learn to take notes in the way that best works for him or her.

There are two important questions to be answered to ensure that you are correctly taking notes:

1. Am I paying attention to and recording the important information?

2. Am I taking notes in a way that best helps me to recall the information for test and quiz preparation?

To answer the first question, you should take notes for a couple of days and then review your notes with your teacher to determine if your teacher feels that you are paying attention to, and making note of, the important information that you will be expected to recall for tests and quizzes.

The answer to the second question requires that you review your notes and determine if they sufficiently jog your memory as to the total scope of the information that was being taught. There are many ways to take notes—from taking shorthand, to drawing pictures, to making mind maps that connect major concepts, to writing short sentences that summarize important topics, terms, or concepts, to using a tape recorder. Whether you use mind maps and lines to connect important concepts, doodle and draw images that help you to recall what the teacher was talking about, or simply write down nearly everything that the teacher says, you must identify the best way for you to make note of the information that is being taught in each of your classes in the way that best helps you to recall what was taught when you review your notes. Experiment with different types of note-taking strategies and review your notes with your teacher, advisor, or counselor to identify the way that is most effective for you.

Step 5: Daily review/summary

The poor study habits of many college students can be traced back to poor study habits that developed when they were in middle school. Do not make this mistake. Get into the habit of taking out your binders and reviewing your class notes each day after school. A few minutes spent reviewing the class notes from each subject will strengthen the connection between memory pathways in your brain. As these pathways  grow stronger, you will experience less difficulty recalling information during tests and quizzes.

The memory pathways that are strengthened from your daily review of your notes will become even stronger if you take the time to draw a picture, compose a rap or poem, or write a paragraph outlining the important concepts covered in each of your classes immediately after reviewing your notes.

Step 6: Review your planner

Performing a daily review of your planner will help to ensure that you do not forget to prepare for scheduled tests and quizzes (provided that you wrote down the test/quiz date in your planner when it was announced by your teacher). It will also help to ensure that you are aware of field trips and changes to the normal class schedule, and that class projects are turned in on time.

Step 7: Test preparation

It follows that if you review your student planner on a daily basis that you are less likely to forget about scheduled tests and quizzes. Taking the time to review your notes and prepare for tests and quizzes represents a level of maturity that many middle school, high school, or even college students fail to develop. Preparation is key to reaching your personal or academic goals.

Step 8: Put your homework where it goes

All of the work in setting up your binders and your homework tabs will be wasted if you do not take the time to place your completed homework into your binders and behind the appropriate tab. Many students get into the bad habit of placing their homework into the pocket in the front of their binders, into their book, or tossing it into their backpacks. If you develop the habit of immediately placing your homework into the respective subject-binder and behind the homework tab as soon as you complete the homework, you will lose and/or misplace fewer homework assignments and receive fewer zeroes for missing homework. As a result you will have higher homework grades!

Step 9: Develop your vocabulary, grammar, and writing skills

Expanding your vocabulary, developing your grammar, and enhancing your writing skills will be critical to high school success, success on college entrance exams such as the SAT and ACT, and ultimately college success. Developing effective written communication skills and understanding the rules of grammar, i.e., correct placement of commas, semi-colons, capitalization, language and word usage will become essential skills in your high school and college-level work.

Successfully expanding your vocabulary and developing your writing skills requires consistent practice, review, correction of errors, and learning how to avoid common errors. The language and writing skills that you develop in middle school will provide the necessary foundation for your high school work and a successful performance on the SAT and/or ACT exams required by most colleges and universities that you may choose to take as a high school sophomore or junior.

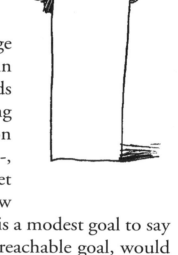

In your Reading, English, or Language Arts subject-binder you should begin developing a vocabulary list of words that will be important to your writing but may not represent the common vocabulary of a typical sixth-, seventh-, or eighth-grade student. You should set a personal goal of identifying one new word during each week of school. This is a modest goal to say the least. A much more aggressive, yet reachable goal, would be to identify one new word each school day.

After identifying a new word:

- write the word onto your vocabulary list;

- write the definition;

- write a sentence using the word; and

- look for an opportunity to use the word in conversation with your friends.

Refer to the *workbook* for a listing of typical words contained on the SAT and/or ACT exams to begin expanding your vocabulary.

Step 10: Become a critical thinker

Step 10: Become a critical thinker

Perhaps the greatest challenge confronting a middle school student is to make decisions based on "thinking" rather than "feelings." Middle school students quickly learn that actions driven by feelings or emotions do not require much thought. Actions that are the result of careful and thoughtful deliberation (critical thinking) take longer and require a good deal more work. Taking the time to engage in the critical thinking process when confronted with decisions pertaining to friends, interactions with parents and teachers, and class work can greatly enhance your overall middle school experience.

The critical thinking process is not very difficult; however, like anything new, it will require some effort on your part. The essence of critical thinking is evaluation, as outlined in the book, *Beyond Feelings: A Guide to Critical Thinking*:

> *The essence of critical thinking is evaluation. Critical thinking, therefore, may be defined as the process by which we test claims and arguments and determine which have merit and which do not. In other words, critical thinking is a search for answers, a quest. Not surprisingly, one of the most important techniques*

used in critical thinking is asking probing questions. Where the uncritical accept their first thought and other people's statements at face value, critical thinkers challenge all ideas.

There are three primary steps involved in the critical thinking process:

- **Investigation:** the process of finding evidence and gathering information. The key to investigation is asking questions and avoiding the inclination to make assumptions.

- **Interpretation:** the process of deciding the facts. After finding evidence, gathering information, and asking questions you must rely upon your thinking skills to process the information that you have gathered in such a way as to formulate opinions, justify positions, recommend solutions, and/or plan a course of action.

- **Judgment:** the process of reaching conclusions as a result of having engaged in the investigative and interpretative phases. Critically thought out conclusions should meet the test of what is logical and/or reasonable.

Review the following characteristics of critical versus uncritical thinkers. Place a check next to those that most reflect how you approach problem-solving or deal with personal or school-related issues. Consciously work toward developing your critical thinking skills and making decisions using the critical thinking process: *investigate, interpret,* and *make a thoughtful judgment.*

Characteristics of critical thinkers versus uncritical thinkers:

Critical Thinkers ...	**Uncritical Thinkers ...**
❏ Are honest with themselves, acknowledging what they do not know, recognizing their own errors.	❏ Pretend they know more than they do, ignore their limitations, and assume their views are error-free.
❏ Regard problems and controversial issues as exciting challenges.	❏ Regard problems and controversial issues as nuisances or threats to their egos.
❏ Base judgments on evidence rather than personal preferences, deferring judgment whenever evidence is insufficient. They revise judgments when new evidence reveals error.	❏ Base judgments on first impressions and gut reactions. They are unconcerned about the amount or quality of evidence and cling to their beliefs steadfastly.
❏ Are interested in other people's ideas and are willing to read and listen attentively, even when they tend to disagree with the other person.	❏ Are preoccupied with themselves and their own opinions, and so are unwilling to pay attention to others' views. At the first sign of disagreement, they tend to think, "How can I prove him wrong?"
❏ Practice restraint, controlling their feelings rather than being controlled by them, and thinking before acting.	❏ Tend to follow their feelings and act impulsively.
❏ Engages in short- and long-term planning based on personal goals and available information relating to achieving personal goals.	❏ Engage in actions driven largely by feelings and emotions. Avoid accepting responsibility for personal failures, lack of effective planning, or not having critically examined available information.

Revisit your dreams

As you consider careers and identify your career dreams, you must consider how what you are learning in school can help you along the road to pursuing your dreams. At this point you may not have a career dream; you may simply dream of attending college, while other students will be more focused on the range of interests and activities which they are pursuing while in school—sports, music, art, dance, or theater. Whatever the case, take time to engage in a classroom discussion about the wide range of career dreams of fellow classmates or talk to your counselor or parent about your possible career dreams and how to use the learning opportunities or programs available at your school to assist you in the pursuit of your career dreams.

Your dream career

When considering a dream career, many students think in terms of money, prestige, and popularity. However, students oftentimes fail to consider the work involved, preparation required, or prospects of actually entering a particular career. For example, many boys aspire to play professional basketball; however, there are over 500,000 high school athletes aspiring toward the same career and fewer than 50 will actually be drafted into the NBA each year; of those 50, less than half will actually make it onto a NBA team. That equates to 500,000 people standing in line for 25 jobs! (ncaa.org)

Revisit college

Now that you have had the opportunity to consider your study skills, ways in which you are smart, ways in which you learn, and who you are, take a moment to ponder what you may like to study in college. For example, while you may love science, you may now realize that you are a very good artist or that you have a real gift for music. This realization does not mean that you have to give up your dreams of becoming a doctor or research scientist,  but that you expand your dreams to include some classes in those areas in which you have other gifts so that you may continue to develop all of your talents.

Revisit careers

The classes that you take in college may prepare you for a broad range of careers. For example, although your primary dream may be to be drafted into the NBA or  WNBA, your college classes in business, psychology, marketing, entrepreneurship, philosophy, and literature will help you to develop a broad range of intellectual and creative gifts. Your hoop dreams may be expanded to include coaching, sports management, uniform design, television analyst, or even team ownership!

Revisit your career dreams each school year as you engage in research activities, take field trips, listen to guest speakers, participate in career days, visit college fairs, and discuss your dreams and aspirations with family, friends, classmates, teachers, counselors, and mentors.

What are your friends' dreams?

As you begin to think about the colleges you may wish to attend and the types of careers you may wish to pursue, take time to talk about your dreams with your friends and/or classmates and ask what their dreams are. Hopefully, you and your friends will support and encourage each other in the pursuit of your respective dreams and career aspirations.

What are your strengths and weaknesses?

It is time for an honest self-assessment. You will probably have many strengths but, painfully, also many weaknesses. Honestly identifying your strengths and weaknesses is an

important step along your journey to becoming the best that you can be. All the other information—personality types, learning styles, Multiple Intelligences, etc.,—has been about helping you to better understand yourself. The same is true of identifying your strengths and weaknesses.

Working toward your dreams and aspirations, whether it be a career, improving your community, or pursuing world peace, will require work, commitment, and knowledge. Achieving your dreams will require that you put forth the effort, make the commitment, and acquire the necessary knowledge. Understanding your strengths and weaknesses is an important step toward identifying the amount of work that will be required and knowledge that will need to be acquired.

What are my strengths and weaknesses in such areas as:

- class work?

- homework?

- preparing for tests and quizzes?

- getting along with others?

- organization?

- note taking?

- subject areas (math, science, etc.)?

- extracurricular activities (sports, clubs, etc.)?

What activities am I involved in after school or on the weekends which help me to develop my strengths?

How and when do I use my basic skills (reading, writing, speaking, mathematics, and listening)?

What things am I doing to increase my basic skills (reading, writing, speaking, mathematics, and listening)?

What ways am I using problem-solving or decision-making skills at school or at home?

What are my three best qualities?

Chapter 4

If you are unable to earn straight A's in every course, the best alternative is often to get top marks in a single area of study. For instance, suppose you love your biochemistry class, but are bored by most of your electives, resulting in only a modest overall GPA. In that case, you are unlikely to win any scholarships that reward overall academic performance. However, with a little extra effort in the class you love, you may be able to distinguish yourself as the top performer in that specific course. Being the best at a particular area of study, no matter how narrowly defined, is often better than being average at everything.

— [The B* Student's Complete Scholarship Book]

Set Goals

Middle school will present an extraordinary opportunity to make new friends, explore new interests, and experience social, emotional, and academic growth. With all that you will be doing and experiencing, you will need a great deal of maturity to maintain your academic focus; yet this is exactly what you must do. Your academic and intellectual development during your three years of middle school will provide the foundation that will greatly influence your high school and college success.

One way to stay focused on your middle school achievement is to set goals and to track your progress during each of your three years. Remember that this is YOUR plan and you are in control of your own effort.

As you will note from the previous chapter, your time during the sixth-through-eighth-grade years will provide an opportunity to begin your transition from a primary-age child through early adolescence as a pre-teen into your first year as an actual teenager. An important part of this transition will be the process of setting and working toward goals.

Counselor/Advisor

Take full advantage of the middle school experience by meeting with your counselor/advisor (or a mentor) to develop a seven-year plan. This plan will include your three years of middle school and your four years of high school. If you are like most middle school students, your plan will undergo many changes and revisions as you experience courses and explore activities. Nevertheless, you must have a plan, you must set goals, and you must work to maintain your focus during your middle and high school years.

Begin by thinking about, discussing, or asking yourself such questions as:

- What are my academic goals during my sixth-, seventh-, and eighth-grade years?

- Would I like to learn to sing and/or play a musical instrument?

- Am I interested in dance, drama, or theater?

- Would I like to enter art shows, athletic events, or theatrical performances?

- Would I like to play on a team or join a club?

- Would I like to represent my school in academic competitions?

- Are there other talents, skills, or areas of interest that I would like to develop or pursue while I am in middle school?

The relationship that you develop with your counselor, advisor, or mentor can make the difference in how fully you take advantage of the middle school experience. Our younger son's middle school (Holcomb Bridge Middle School in Alpharetta, Georgia) developed a program called GATE (Gifts, Abilities, Talents, and Excellence). Through their program they helped students better understand themselves (as outlined in Chapter One). Students met with faculty advisors to identify their intellectual gifts (i.e., Multiple Intelligences) and interests. Each faculty advisor, meeting with a small group of students, is helping students to not only get to know themselves but to more fully take advantage of the wide range of opportunities available in middle school, and eventually at the high school that students will ultimately attend. Whether or not your school has a formal program such as GATE, there are steps that you can take to build such a relationship with your counselor, advisor, or mentor:

1. Take the information that you gathered in Chapter One: *Understand Who You Are* and share it with your counselor, advisor, or mentor.

2. Ask him or her to assist you in identifying opportunities within your school and community to further explore your areas of interest.

3. Ask him or her to assist you in developing your seven-year middle-through-high school plan of academics and extracurricular activities.

Remember that whatever you learn, and activities that you explore, in middle school will prepare you for high school; both schools are part of your overall college plan.

What are the opportunities?

Many students find it difficult to set goals when they enter middle school. They are so excited and apprehensive about middle school itself that for them their primary goals are simply attending school and making friends. While attending school is undoubtedly important and making friends should certainly be part of the middle school experience, middle school offers a wide range of academic, social, athletic, artistic, musical, and special-interest opportunities for personal growth and development that may inspire your future dreams and aspirations. To ensure that you take advantage of the full range of opportunities you must gather information in regards to the complete scope of the programs and activities available at your middle school. This will include clubs, before- and after-school programs, athletics, local, national, and intraschool competitions, mentoring/ tutorial opportunities, and the full range

of extracurricular activities from the Jr. Beta Club to intramural sports.

In addition to those programs and activities offered at your middle school and within your community, there is likely to be a broad range of programs, activities, and

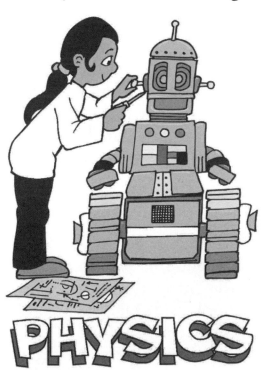

camps offered during the summer months. Many middle schoolers feel that they are too old for summer camps, however, parents and students should take advantage of the opportunity to explore as many programs as possible. Our younger son attended the Summer Institute for the Gifted at Emory University in Atlanta, Georgia during the summer between sixth and seventh grades. During the camp he built robots, performed in a musical, tried a court case, and learned how to become a life guard. Such programs provide excellent opportunities to further explore your interests and develop your skills and talents.

Develop an academic schedule

Getting to college will require that you successfully complete middle school. Your three years of middle school coursework should prepare you for a successful high school experience. With a focus on college, you should already be thinking about the classes you will take in high school, the clubs and student organizations in which you will be involved, and the extracurricular activities and volunteer hours to which you will commit. By eleventh grade, what you have done will determine whether or not you have made yourself a competitive candidate for admissions into your first-choice colleges.

Creating a seven-year course schedule will require that you investigate the programs and activities available at the high school that you will be attending. A sixth-grade student certainly does not have to make a commitment to one high school or the other; however, this is the time to begin gathering information, talking to other students, and thinking about which high school you may be interested in attending. Your decision may very well be influenced by the programs and/or activities offered at the school.

For the sixth-grade student, eighth grade appears a lifetime away. However, it will come a lot faster than you think and when it does come, you will have to choose a high school academic course of study (i.e., track) that you will have to commit to for your four years of high school. In a general sense the course of study will either be college preparatory or directed toward a trade or vocation. As a beginning ninth-grade student, you may think that your ultimate career or vocational interest will be in a trade such as construction, masonry, or cosmetology; however, four years of high school will provide

ample opportunity to reconsider your choice and/or change your mind. While you may have some flexibility during your high school years in changing your course of study, you may find it difficult to change from a vocational track to a college preparatory track. It may be easier to choose college and change your mind to working a trade, vocation, or attending a trade or technical school after high school than the reverse. In fact, some high schools offer dual diplomas (college preparatory and trade/technical) which allow students to choose both a vocational and a college preparatory track.

In any event, you must sit down with your middle and high school counselors to identify the classes necessary to keep you on course toward your dreams and aspirations.

A recent analysis by the U.S. Department of Education indicates that high school students who take algebra, geometry, and other rigorous mathematics courses are more likely to go on to college. .

The key to understanding mathematics is taking algebra or courses covering algebraic concepts by the end of the eighth grade. Achievement at that stage gives students an important advantage in taking rigorous high school mathematics and science courses. However, many eighth- and ninth-graders may already be <u>behind</u> in their course selection to get on to the road to college. Some schools do not offer everyone a full selection of challenging courses, or because not all students are prepared for and encouraged to enroll. The results of the recent Third International Mathematics and Science Study (TIMSS) confirm that many students enter high school without a solid grounding in mathematics, closing doors very early for further education and better careers.

[U.S. Department of Education: Mathematics Equals Opportunity]

Developing a good middle school and high school plan will certainly help you to get into college; however, you must keep in mind that your ultimate goal is not simply to get into college but to *graduate from college*. This means that you must be capable of completing the college coursework. Now is the time to begin thinking about preparing yourself to take the most academically challenging high school classes which you are capable of performing well in. The more academically challenging high school classes will provide the skills, training, knowledge, and academic foundation that will help you to succeed in even more difficult college classes (depending on your college major or type of degree you will be working toward). By preparing for, and taking, the most academically challenging classes in high school, many students discover that they are so well prepared that some of their college courses are actually easier than their high school classes.

Middle school is the time for you to explore your interests, discover your passions, develop your gifts, and identify the subjects and activities that you enjoy. While you can always change your mind, choose different careers, or pursue different interests, you should begin to identify those areas where you have passionate interests versus those areas where you have very little interest. Keep in mind that if you are going to spend four years or more in college that you should be taking classes and engaged in an area where you have a passion to learn or be involved in pursuing a career where you will enjoy the work. Ultimately, the career path that you begin pursuing through your college studies will be one that may last through the majority of your adult life. It is better to move in the direction of an area of study or a career that you love now as opposed to one that you will hate later! Now is the time to begin to explore your interests as you continue to discover who you are and what you enjoy doing.

High school credit

Some middle school courses can receive high school credit. For example, many school districts award high school credit for two years of a foreign language taken in middle school. The requirements to receive high school credit for classes taken in middle school will vary by school district. Some school districts require a certain grade in the class and require that the class be taken in consecutive years. Other school districts award high school credit for 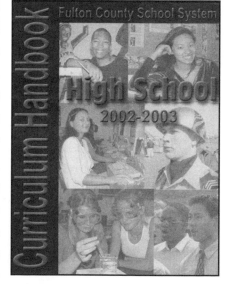 such middle school math classes as Algebra I and Geometry when students fulfill either academic grade requirements or achieve a certain score on an End-of-Course-Test. Our older son received high school credit for Spanish I by taking three consecutive years of Spanish in middle school. This allowed him to take Spanish II as a ninth-grader and ultimately AP Spanish, the highest level of Spanish offered in his school district, as an eleventh-grader in high school. Our younger son is on track to take Algebra I and Spanish I during middle school. Review your school district's middle school and high school course catalogs and meet with your middle school counselor, and eventually a high school counselor, to identify the classes necessary to keep you on course toward fulfilling your college-bound plan.

Grades

Middle school will provide many challenges and opportunities for academic growth and development. You will have multiple teachers and subjects. As you might  imagine, academic success is one of the important components of your college plan. Not only will your grades be an important indicator of your ability to succeed in college-level work, but the knowledge, problem-solving skills, and writing and language skills that you develop by applying yourself in your classes will all become important pieces of the overall academic foundation, preparation, and knowledge base that you will draw upon during your college studies.

No matter what level of academic achievement you experienced in elementary school, you must now set your goals for your middle school grades. Each time that you receive your middle school class schedule, set an academic goal for each class and write down the grade that you would like to achieve next to the class. You must work as hard as you can to pass every class, achieve the grade that you set out to achieve, and perform to the best of your abilities throughout middle school. You will discover that your effort and commitment to perform at your best will provide the foundation for high school success, and later, college success.

Standardized tests

All middle school students are required to take various standardized and/or End-of-Course tests. School districts use these tests to assess what you are learning and how well you are performing in school. You should take preparation and performance on these mandatory tests seriously. They may influence what type of academic classes you can take, whether you are placed into academically gifted or remedial classes, whether or not you can take higher-level math or science classes, and in some school districts whether or not you are promoted to the next grade!

If you are not a good test taker, then you are going to have to develop better test-taking skills. Your performance on such tests may impact the academic opportunities that you have in your school district. Eventually, colleges are going to evaluate you, in part, based on your performance on standardized tests.

If you were a baseball player and could not hit a curve ball, what would you do? Practice hitting curve balls. If you were a wide receiver and could not catch passes, what would you do? Practice catching passes. If you were a quarterback and could not throw the ball properly, what would you do? Practice throwing the ball. If you experienced difficulty shooting free throws, what would you do? You guessed it. You would practice shooting free throws. If you do not do well on tests, you have to practice and develop better test-taking skills. Failure is not an option!

Taking your tests seriously requires that you review and track all of your test scores. After reviewing your test scores, consciously work to expand your strengths and develop plans to improve upon your weaknesses. If you have low reading scores, read more and spend time with a reading specialist or someone who can help you learn how to read  better. If you have low math scores, get a tutor and enroll in more challenging math classes to increase your math knowledge and skill level.

Never be ashamed of your current knowledge or ability level. If you struggle in reading or in understanding/ performing mathematical computations, you must be honest with yourself and your teachers. Teachers are there to help but they cannot give you the amount of help that you need if you are not honest in letting them know when you are having difficulty.

Community involvement, social clubs, or religious involvement

You may already be involved in a church choir, youth program, of other type of faith-based or community program. Consider which programs or activities you may wish to continue throughout middle school, later in high school, and ultimately during college. An important part of your college application will be your community involvement.

Extracurricular activities

Many students become involved in organized sports in elementary school. Middle school is a good time to either continue your involvement in organized sports or to  become involved as a means of preparing yourself for high school sports competition. Would you like to compete in AAU (Amateur Athletic Union) basketball, track and field, wrestling, gymnastics, soccer, baseball, or martial arts? Are you interested in soccer, lacrosse, swimming, or tennis? Your involvement in organized sports, with good coaching, can prepare you for high school competition, which in turn, prepares you to become a college athlete. Young people who are involved in youth sports programs in elementary and middle school tend to have more success in high school sports. High school coaches think highly of youth development programs that help young people develop their fundamental skills and knowledge of practice routines, game strategy, and the requirements for high school level competition.

If you are considering competing in a sport in high school it would be advisable for you to visit the high school and speak with the coach. Ask the coach what you can do during middle school to prepare yourself.

In addition to sports, take advantage of the middle school opportunities for involvement in band, orchestra, student government, theater, math, art, science or speech and debate competitions, and interschool scholastic competitions.

Summer camps/enrichment

During the summers while you are in middle school, explore the opportunities for enrolling in summer programs. There are usually summer programs in the arts, music, math and science. Such programs provide excellent opportunities to explore your interests and prepare for high school success.

If you have already identified areas of interest, e.g., sports, art, science, mathematics, modeling, acting, sailing, etc., enrolling in summer camps, and/or competing in local and national competitions will provide invaluable opportunities to further develop your talent and gain exposure to a level 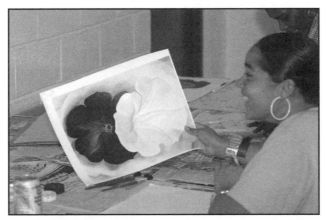 of competition that will help you to prepare for high school. Talk to other students, teachers, and parents as you gather information about summer camps and programs.

Before- after-school programs

Before- and/or after-school programs provide further opportunities to explore your interests or expand upon your musical, artistic, athletic, or academic gifts. Participation in such programs may help develop your high school focus or even help you to make your decision as to which high school you will apply to. Current high school graduation requirements include a specified number of community service hours and extracurricular activity participation.

Awards

Talk to your counselors and teachers about the complete scope of awards and recognition that you can earn during your three years of middle school. The available awards will vary from those that you compete for in academic, athletic, artistic, dance, and musical competitions to those where you are recognized for attendance, citizenship, student government, or participation in school and community programs.

After identifying the full range of awards and recognition opportunities, set goals and identify the awards or type of recognition you would like to earn and make note of them onto the worksheets in the *workbook*.

Middle school achievements

Place copies of all of the newspaper articles, honor roll certificates, athletic accomplishments, or other awards that you receive during middle school into your *College Plan* binder and/or grade-level box (i.e., sixth grade, seventh grade, or eighth grade) as soon as you receive the award.

If the award is being given by someone who knows you personally, ask if he or she would write a letter of recommendation and place a copy into your binder.

Staff connections

Many middle school students experience some difficulty in the beginning as they discover that middle school teachers are oftentimes more demanding than elementary school teachers. Some students even accuse their teachers of being mean. You must accept the fact that you are going to have more teachers, take more subjects, have more homework, and be expected to be more independent and

personally responsible than you experienced in elementary school. However, keep in mind that your teachers are there to help you and it is in your own best interest to develop positive relationships with your teachers. The easiest way to accomplish this is to avoid making assumptions like, "My

teacher doesn't like me;" instead, take the time to talk with and get to know your teachers. Share your college aspirations with your teachers and ask them to share some of their college experiences with you. Developing positive relationships with your teachers, counselors, and administrators will allow them to help you navigate your way through middle school, into high school, and ultimately into college.

Policies and procedures

To take full advantage of the range of middle school opportunities, you have to take your middle school policies and procedures seriously. Discipline infractions not only disrupt the middle school experience for classmates, interfere with classroom instruction, and contribute negatively to your school's overall school climate and culture but may cause you

This will serve as a reminder of where the information that has been outlined in this chapter should be filed:

- During the first days of school, as you receive your class schedule, course syllabus, and other important papers, file them in the appropriate binder or box as soon as you receive them.

- Place your worksheets and seven-year course schedule into your college-planning binder.

- Place copies of your awards and certificates into the appropriate box (i.e., sixth-, seventh-, or eighth-grade box).

- Record your standardized tests and/or EOCT scores onto your worksheets and place the tests into the appropriate box.

to forfeit your opportunity to participate in extracurricular activities, field trips, assemblies, or limit your involvement in before- or after-school programs.

Perhaps the most difficult values for middle school students to understand and to accept are respect and responsibility. Learning how to respect the adults and students in your school and being responsible for completing your work and living up to the school's expectations of student behaviors will provide the foundation for you to experience the entire range of programs and opportunities. Your attitude and behavior will have a tremendous impact on your school community and on your opportunity to experience an enlightening, inspiring, and personally rewarding middle school experience.

End-of-year assessment

At the end of the school year you should take time to do an honest assessment of your efforts and how well you did in achieving your goals. Doing so will allow you an opportunity for self-reflection over the summer. While you probably would rather forget about school altogether, you must stay focused on your plan and continue your efforts to recognize your strengths and weaknesses.

Teacher assessment

Take a moment to reflect on teachers, counselors, tutors, and coaches. Identify those who really helped you as well as those with whom you had challenges. How did their personality,

behavior, or teaching style contribute to either a positive or less than positive relationship? How did these individuals affect what you learned in their class or how you performed on their teams?

Chapter 5

Studying and being a serious student take time and persistence, not pure genius. When I keep emphasizing repetition, I'm not saying this idly—very few students skim a textbook quickly and then master the material. The adage that genius is 99 percent perspiration and 1 percent inspiration is remarkably astute. Most students I saw who were considering applying to Ivy League schools were those who were both interested in learning and had dedicated a great portion of their lives to learning.

— Michele A. Hernandez [The Middle School Years]

Middle—High School Transition

The book, *"A High School Plan for Students with College-Bound Dreams,"* will help you to explore and to develop a complete high school strategy. What is important to note here is that few middle school students are thinking about college when they enter middle school and worst yet, few are thinking about college when they enter high school! The question that students should be asking themselves upon entering high school (which they in all probability will not even think of) is, "Four years from now, why would a college want to accept my application into their freshman class? What will be special about me and what will I be able to contribute to their school community?"

Asking those questions now will help you to begin the process of becoming—becoming a teacher, artist, scholar, musician, scientist, mathematician, entrepreneur, computer programmer, leader, athlete, or web site designer. Taking advantage of your middle school opportunities and exploring a wide range of classes and interests will help to focus and prepare you for your eventual middle-to-high school transition.

Students often find the transition from eighth grade to ninth grade a difficult one. Some students may even consider ninth grade to be the most difficult year of their lives. On the  contrary, the transition into high school is just another step in your college-bound plan. Growing into a young adult will require that you carefully consider the actions that you take in resolving conflicts, and there will be many. You are likely to experience conflicts with your parents, siblings, teachers, and classmates. You will be confronted with deciding which groups of students to identify and socialize with. As was the case when entering into middle school, you will experience mounting peer pressure and conflicting advice as your friends lead you into one direction while parents, teachers, and other adults push or encourage you into other directions.

Sixth-grade students who find themselves among the smallest and least mature students in their middle schools are more likely to try to avoid conflicts, whereas ninth-grade students try to fit in immediately and frequently put themselves in the middle of conflicts. Those ninth-graders who are smart enough to avoid conflicts too frequently are not smart enough to choose the right friends. Your friends are more likely to encourage you to misbehave rather than to do the right thing. They are more likely to encourage you not to do your  homework and prepare for tests than to do your best. They are more likely to encourage you to cut school, do drugs, drink alcohol, smoke cigarettes (or marijuana), or have sex, exactly the opposite of what your parents want you to do.

As a ninth-grade student, new to the high school environment, you will have to work hard at effectively resolving conflicts and avoiding discipline infractions. Discipline infractions are taken seriously by college admission committees and in many cases will cause your application to be denied outright. Hopefully, the three years of developing your critical thinking skills during your time in middle school will provide you with the intellectual ability, problem-solving skills, and common sense to experience a smooth transition into high school.

Despite the need to be with your friends, you do not have to pull away from your parent(s). Your relationship with your parent(s) is going to change but it does not have to change for the worst. You can hang out with your little demons—pardon me, friends—without severing your relationship with your parent(s).

Independent decision making

My wife and I have what we believe to be a strong relationship with our older son, who survived both middle school and high school (just barely!) and is currently attending college, and our younger son who is in the seventh grade. The phrase that we use in our home is "IDM" which means "Independent Decision Making." Rather than blindly following the advice of friends, who rarely know more than they do, they should be *IDMing*—using their own critical thinking skills to be independent decision makers. We know that their friends use language of which we would not approve, talk about things of which we would not approve, and do things of which we would not approve. By talking to our sons, they know that my wife and I know. As parents, we do not compromise our values or lower our expectations because their friends have different values and/or lower expectations.

Are you an independent decision maker or do you tend to follow the crowd? Did your behavior this school year reflect leadership skills or poor decision making based on peer pressure or the need to follow the crowd? As you reflect on the school year, were you *IDMing*—using your own critical-thinking skills to be an independent decision maker? Were your actions guided by your own sense of right and wrong or did you find yourself getting into unnecessary trouble as a result of poor decisions or negative influence of peers?

Identify people to whom you can talk

Some students will have a smooth transition from middle school to high school, but many others will find the transition particularly difficult. They may find themselves struggling academically, uncomfortable socially, and lost in the sea of faces. Typically, high school represents the largest school setting that entering students have experienced and is not well suited to the personality types of many students.

All young people are under similar pressure "How do I become the person whom my parents expect me to be and fit in with my friends?" Consider that no matter how much you and your parent(s) disagree about hairstyles, clothes, body piercing, tattoos, music, friends, school, or life itself, you can still maintain a close relationship with your  parent(s). While many of your friends may appear to be the most important people in your life, they are in your life for only a short period of time. Years from now you will have moved on, made new friends, and lost touch with most of today's friends; however, your parent(s) will be there for a lifetime. They have a huge role in your college plan and your relationship with them should be one that you can rely upon as you work through your middle school plan.

Enjoy your time in school and stay focused on your future. Discover your dreams and pursue life's extraordinary opportunities.

Set your sails toward high school

Ideally, you should begin familiarizing yourself with the four critical areas of your high school plan no later than at the beginning of eighth grade:

- Academics

- Extracurricular Activities

- Personal Qualities

- Intangibles

You should also begin working through the activities in the book and workbook, *A High School Plan for Students with College-Bound Dreams* to ensure that you are prepared for high school and that your ninth-grade course schedule is consistent with your overall college-bound plan.

Chapter 6

Begin with the end in mind! Focus on the wonderful, magnificent, intelligent, educated person that you see your child becoming and work backwards. For example, if you see your child becoming a doctor, then help her to walk, speak, and behave responsibly like a doctor, today. Help her to begin developing the character of a good doctor, today. Begin using and spelling medical terms at home, today. Get your preschooler a doctor's kit. Get your elementary child a medical dictionary and encyclopedia. Get your middle school child a microscope and a listing of medical schools. Get your high school student familiar with college applications and admissions requirements as he or she enters into high school. Your daughter should know what test scores, grades, and student activities are required to help her compete for admittance into the colleges that will best prepare her to enter into the medical school of her choice. Now is the time to focus on qualifying for a college scholarship.

— *Mychal Wynn*
[Ten Steps to Helping Your Child Succeed in School]

A Final Word to Parents

It would be great if, as a parent, you could simply give this book and the *workbook* to your child, sit back and watch him or her work through each of the chapters, identify their strengths and weaknesses, plan their course schedule, track their grades and test scores, and remain focused during their three years of middle school. However, such is rarely the case. Some children require your prodding, support, encouragement, and hands-on involvement throughout the entire seven-year period encompassing middle and high school. Some children will even require your active involvement throughout the four years of college.

As children undergo the broad range of physical and emotional changes associated with their journey through early adolescence into their teenage years, on more than one occasion parents are likely to question, "Is this my child?" Parents are likely to experience emotions from joy to depression; attitudes from encouraging to unbelievably negative; behaviors from polite to rebellious; and character traits from truthfulness to unconscionable deceit! Perhaps, most perplexing to parents is that psychologists will advise you that this is all normal and to be expected!

Unfortunately, a parent's responsibility for school success during the important middle and high school years does not stop at the school door. Nor, is there a particular school year in which your child can be considered, "All grown up" and therefore not require any more attention on your part. Some children will require little monitoring while others will require daily, and in some instances, hourly monitoring. Some children will require little interaction with their teachers while others will require that you communicate with their teachers on a frequent, if not daily basis. On more than one occasion, as parents, we have thrown our hands up in frustration after logging on to our school's grading system to discover that our son has  missed countless assignments, failed to turn in homework that we worked with him all weekend to ensure that he completed, and 'forgot' to inform us of a major class project due the next day!

Helping your child successfully navigate his or her way through the middle through high school years will require diligence, determination, perseverance and patience on your part driven by your love for your child and your unwavering belief in his or her potential. To enhance your child's middle school experience and pave the way to his or her academic and social success lets review your role in each of the previous chapters.

The academic battlefield

Students today are more likely to be found playing a video game than a musical instrument; watching television than reading a book; and more concerned about how they look than what their grades are. Many households are engaged in a daily battle between parents who want their children to apply themselves toward their school work and children who are intent on learning new video game codes, talking on the telephone, or socializing in Internet chat rooms.

Despite this daily tug-of-war, parents must not waiver in their determination to lead their children if possible or to force them if necessary, to read, write, think, and compute. Some of the strategies that you may consider are:

- Eliminate television between Sunday evening and Thursday evening.

- Ask teachers for recommended books and develop an at-home library.

- Require your children to read daily.

- Pack up video games during the school year and limit their use to summer and holidays.

- Require your children to write: notes, letters, to-do lists, poetry, short stories—just write.

- Require your children to think: solve brain teasers, math equations, conduct science experiments, plan grocery shopping, compute the household budget, put together a puzzle, build models, etc.

- Connect your child's social opportunities (e.g., telephone calls, movies, parties, etc.) to their academic performance.

- Place report cards and test scores in a conspicuous location (e.g., the refrigerator) so that your entire family is focused on academic achievement and supporting the academic success of everyone in the family.

- Never say anything disparaging about school, education, or educators around your children. If you have a problem, communicate directly with the school or school teacher in question.

Complete activities and forms together

The importance that you place on education is best communicated by example. Complete the forms, activities, and worksheets in the *workbook* with your child. Learn to listen to their dreams, encourage their aspirations, and celebrate their effort. Academic achievement is most often the result of effort. The effort of the student who  works diligently to raise a grade from 'D' to 'C' is to be celebrated as much as that of the student who raises a grade from 'B' to 'A.' Completing the activities and worksheets together will allow you and your child to see patterns and trends in their grades and test scores.

Chapter 1: Understand Who You Are

Understanding your child's personality, learning style, and identifying his or her intellectual strengths and weaknesses will be as important to you as it will be to him or her. If you have more than one child they are likely to be different from each other. One may be highly organized while the other is totally unorganized. One may be introverted while the other talks all of the time. One may effortlessly do his or her school work while the other finds him or herself frequently struggling. It will be important for you and your children to learn to appreciate and celebrate each other's unique gifts and to work together as a family to assist each other in overcoming or strengthening their weaknesses.

Understanding the uniqueness of each child will also assist greatly in developing an effective system of rewards and consequences. You can be assured that during the middle school and into the high school years that the only way to effectively deal with student apathy and the consistent lack of responsible behavior is to "encourage" them through a system of effective consequences!

Chapter 2: Why College?

It is important for your child to continually hear the college message at home. You must reinforce to him or her that the middle school and high school years are designed to lead him or her into college. His or her work, attitude, and school involvement is all part of a larger plan, their plan, designed to get into and succeed in college. You should follow the advice in chapter one and get yourself and your household organized for the seven-year journey through middle and high school.

Chapter 3: Elementary—Middle School Transition

A successful transition from elementary to middle school will require that you establish open lines of communication with your child's teachers. Ensuring that your child gets off to a good start in middle school and successfully transitions between the adolescence changes during the  sixth-, seventh-, and eighth-grade years will require that you maintain the frequency of home-school communication that is appropriate for your child. Some children require infrequent communication with their teachers while other children require weekly, if not daily, parent-teacher communication.

Some of the important challenges that you may experience are:

- ensuring that your child stays organized

- ensuring that your child brings home the necessary books and materials to complete homework and/or class projects

- ensuring that your child completes and turns in homework on time

- ensuring that you are aware of when tests and quizzes are being given and that your child adequately prepares

- being aware in a timely manner of your child's classroom participation and completion of class work

- being aware of any behaviors that may be interfering with your child's classroom success

- being aware of the negative impact of peer pressures

Dealing with these types of challenges will require that you:

1. Talk to your child on a daily basis about school, school work, and school activities.

2. Develop effective at-home routines to help your child stay focused on his or her school responsibilities and to help you effectively monitor homework completion and test preparation.

3. Identify the most effective way to communicate with teachers.

4. Take a proactive approach to identifying problem areas and meeting with teachers to develop strategies to ensure your child's academic and social success.

Do not be lulled into a false sense of security that the transition from elementary to middle school automatically brings with it maturity and responsibility. These will come eventually, however, you cannot assume that either will come automatically, if at all, during the middle school years.

Chapter 4: Set Goals

You are likely to find that your children effortlessly establish goals that are important to them, such as:

- reaching new levels on their video games,

- recording certain television programs,

- scheduling trips to the mall, or

- planning to attend movies or concerts.

You are also likely to find that the last thing on your child's mind will be to establish the goals that are necessary for school success, such as:

- recording assignments, test, and quiz announcements in their planner

- completing and turning in their class work and homework consistently and on time

- effectively preparing for tests and quizzes

- putting forth the necessary effort to complete quality class projects

- consistently qualifying for Honor Roll and achieving the highest standardized test scores

It would be ideal if students established and engaged in the diligent pursuit of their own academic goals, however, failing this, parents have to establish goals that are in their child's best interest. Establishing academic and social goals for your  child is needed until your child achieves the maturity and responsibility level to independently establish and pursue his or her own goals. While qualifying for the Honor Roll or Principal's List are worthy academic goals, keep in mind that being recognized for academic achievement is a secondary goal—the primary goal is learning. Qualifying for academic honors is a by-product of the effort put forth and the learning itself. Recognition for demonstrating the core values or good citizenship at school is a by-product of demonstrating the character and behavior that brings honor to a student's family and school.

Helping your child to develop personal goals during his or her middle and high school years will enable him or her to understand the importance of establishing personal and professional goals well into their young adult lives and beyond.

Chapter 5: Middle—High School Transition

If you use this book, perform the activities, complete the worksheets in the *workbook*, and remain patient, yet persistent, in helping your child to develop the character, study habits, organizational skills, and personal focus on school today and college tomorrow, the transition from middle school into high school will be a successful one for your child and for your family. The strain of the middle school years do not have to be unbearable and the undeniable changes that young people undergo during their middle school years can and should be a largely enjoyable one for the student and his or her family. The middle school years should be filled with experiences that a family can reflect back on in celebration rather than trepidation. However, ensuring an enjoyable and effective learning experience during your child's middle school years will require that you accept your role in guiding him or her along their journey.

Be assured that students are less inclined to want their parents involved at school during their middle school years and oftentimes are downright discouraging of any parental involvement during their high school years. However, it is during a student's middle and high school years that they are most in need of active parental involvement as they are being confronted with difficult and confusing decisions associated with their journey through early adolescence and emergence into puberty. While your child is less inclined to discuss these important issues with you; less inclined to want to spend time with you; and less inclined to share the important issues of peer pressures and infatuation with others this is the time when they will need to know that you are available and willing to listen. On the following page is a list of five important things to practice as your child continues on his or her journey.

Additional resources that you will need to ensure that your child has a comprehensive seven-year college-bound plan are:

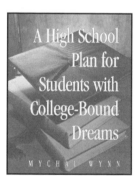

- *Ten Steps to Helping Your Child Succeed in School* [Wynn/Rising Sun Publishing]

- *A High School Plan for Students with College-Bound Dreams* [Wynn/Rising Sun Publishing]

- *A High School Plan for Students with College-Bound Dreams: Workbook* [Wynn/Rising Sun Publishing]

5 Steps to Surviving Middle School for Parents and Students

1. Take time each day to listen to each other.

2. Establish ground rules for engaging in meaningful discussions where both parent and student can openly and calmly share ideas and opinions.

3. Establish high academic, social, and behavioral expectations despite popular trends and changing societal norms.

4. Communicate expectations, identify responsibilities, and establish rewards/consequences.

5. Exercise patience, avoid excuses, and take the time to think before you speak!

Glossary

As you begin and continue through the college-planning process, you will find references to many unfamiliar terms in regards to college admissions, financial aid, standardized tests, and coursework. The intent of this Glossary is to provide a comprehensive listing of the terminology pertaining to the college admissions process.

3-2 Liberal Arts and Career Combination: A program in which a student completes three years of study in a liberal arts field followed by two years of professional technical study (i.e., engineering, forestry, architecture, etc.), at the end of which the student is awarded the Bachelor of Arts by the first institution and Bachelor of Science degree by the second.

568 Group: The 568 Group is made up of 28 of the top colleges in the United States, including Amherst College, the University of Chicago, Columbia, Duke, Georgetown, Rice, Stanford, and Yale universities. (Four of the Ivies are not participating: Brown, Dartmouth, Harvard, and Princeton.) The group, named after a law that waives antitrust provisions to allow the members to meet, wants to lessen the confusing variation in financial-aid offers by requiring financial-aid officers to use the same method for determining a student's financial need.

AA (Associate of Arts): A degree which is granted to a student who has completed a two-year program (64-66 credits) in liberal arts and is equivalent to the first two years of study for a bachelor's degree.

AAS (Associate of Applied Science): A degree that is granted to students who have completed a technology or vocational program. It is generally considered a terminal degree as it prepares students for immediate employment upon graduation. In some cases, the credits earned while completing an AAS can be transferred to a bachelor's degree, but only when specified by the school or program in question.

Academic Year: A period of time that schools use to measure a quantity of study. Academic years vary from school to school and even from educational program to educational program within the same school.

Academic Index: A formula used by schools to index rank/grades and test scores to quickly compare applications.

Acceptance Form: This form documents the student's receipt of an award letter. The form usually includes a space to indicate acceptance of offered financial aid, declination of all or part of the package and some means for requesting an appeal to modify the award. Acceptance letters and award letters are frequently combined into a single document.

ACT (American College Testing Exam): The ACT Assessment is a curriculum-based college admissions test. This means that the multiple choice questions on the ACT are a measure of what you have learned in your high school classes rather than aptitude or I.Q. The ACT tests the four subject areas of: English, Mathematics, Reading, and Science Reasoning with an optional writing test. ACT results are accepted by most U.S. colleges.

- **English:** 75-question, 45-minute test that measures your understanding of the conventions of standard written English (punctuation, grammar and usage, and sentence structure) and of rhetorical skills (strategy, organization, and style).
- **Mathematics:** 60-question, 60-minute test designed to assess the mathematical skills students have typically acquired in courses taken up to the beginning of 12th grade. Use of calculators is permitted.
- **Reading:** 40-question, 35-minute test that measures your reading comprehension.
- **Science:** 40-question, 35-minute test that measures the interpretation, analysis, evaluation, reasoning, and problem-solving skills required in the natural sciences.

A perfect score is 36.

Admit: You got in!

Admit-Deny: Some schools will admit marginal students, but not award them any financial aid. Very few schools use admit-deny, because studies have shown that lack of sufficient financial aid is a key factor in the performance of marginal students.

All-American: A high school athlete who is one of the best in the country and is usually recruited.

All-county/All-state: A high school athlete who is one of the best in the county or state.

AP (Advanced Placement): The AP program is managed by the College Board. The AP program consists of over 30 courses that lead up to an examination, given in May of each year, that can, depending on a student's score, result in college credit. AP courses are generally looked upon favorably by college admissions officers as evidence of a challenging high school program. AP exam scores range from 0 to 5. Scores above 3 are considered passing and may be eligible for college credit; however, individual colleges have their own procedures and requirements for awarding credit for AP exams. Some colleges will award credit based on the AP exam score; other colleges do not offer credit but may award advanced standing based on the scores and number of AP exams taken.

AP Scholar: Recipients of the AP Scholar Award are notified in the fall following the May exam.

AP Scholar: Grades of 3 or higher on 3 or more AP Exams on full-year courses.

AP Scholar with Honor: Average grade of 3.25 on all AP exams taken, and grades of 3 or higher on 4 or more of these exams on full-year courses.

AP Scholar with Distinction: Average grade of at least 3.5 on all AP Exams taken, and grades of 3 or higher on 5 or more of these exams on full-year courses.

AP State Scholar: One female and one male student in each U.S. state and the District of Columbia with the highest average grade (at least 3.5) on all AP Exams taken, and grades of 3 or higher on the greatest number of exams. The minimum requirement is a grade of 3 or higher on 3 exams on full-year courses.

National AP Scholar: Students in the United States who receive an average grade of at least 4 on all AP Exams taken, and grades of 4 or higher on 8 or more of these exams on full-year courses.

Department of Defense for Education Activity (DoDEA) Scholar: One female and one male student attending DoDEA schools with the highest average grade on the greatest number of AP Exams. The minimum requirement is a grade of 3 or higher on 3 exams on full-year courses.

AP International Scholar: One male and one female student attending an American international school (that is not a DoDEA school) outside the U.S. and Canada with the highest average grade on the greatest number of AP Exams. The minimum requirement is a grade of 3 or higher on 3 exams on full-year courses.

Alma mater: Latin for "soul mother." This is the term used to refer to the college from which a person graduated.

Articulation Agreements: Agreements between colleges offering two-year programs that allow for students to continue their studies at a four-year university.

AS (Associate of Science): A degree which is granted to a student who has completed a two-year program (64-66 credits) in the sciences and is equivalent to the first two years of study for a bachelor's degree.

ASVAB (Armed Services Vocational Aptitude Test Battery): Armed Services Vocational Aptitude Test Battery is specifically designed to identify individual aptitude in five career areas. Branches of military service use these results to determine eligibility for entrance and job training placement. This battery of tests is given at each high school and is open without cost to any senior.

Award Letter: The form which notifies the student that financial aid is being offered. The award letter usually provides information about the types and amounts of aid offered, as well as specific program information, student responsibilities and the conditions which govern the award. The Award Letter often includes an Acceptance Form.

Award Year: The time beginning on July 1 of one year and extending to June 30 of the next year.

BA (Bachelor of Arts): A degree which is granted to a student who has completed a four-year program (120-128 credits) in the liberal arts.

Base Year: The U.S. Federal tax year used for analyzing student financial need. **The base year is the calendar year preceding the award year.**

BS (Bachelor of Science): A degree which is granted to a student who has completed a four-year program (120-128 credits) in the sciences.

Campus-Based Programs: The term commonly applied to those U.S. Department of Education federal student aid programs administered directly by institutions of postsecondary education. Includes: Federal Perkins Loan, Federal Supplemental Educational Opportunity Grant (FSEOG) and Federal Work-Study (FWS) programs.

Candidate's Reply Date: May 1 has been designated by the College Board as the date by which a student must make a commitment to the college he or she will attend in the fall. Many schools will notify a student of admission before April 15 (the last day the colleges must inform students about their applications).

Career Office: The office that provides student assistance ranging from résumé tips to interview techniques to finding an internship, it's the place to go for anything related to finding a job.

Carnegie Unit: The unit was developed in the United States in 1906 as a measure of the amount of time a student has studied a subject. Most U.S. high school classes earn the equivalent of 1 Carnegie unit per semester.

CCA (Collegiate Commissioners Association): The Collegiate Commissioners Association administers the National Letter of Intent program. There are specific National Letter of Intent signing dates established each year. Contact the NLI office at 205.458.3000 or check the NLI web site at *www.national-letter.org*.

CEEB (College Entrance Examination Board): Administers the SAT I and SAT II examinations.

Class Rank: A student's position in his or her graduating class. Most ranks are expressed as a fraction; for example, your rank may be 5/400, which would mean you graduated 5th in a class of 400. In some states, class rank may be the single deciding factor for admissions into the state university system.

CLEP (College-Level Examination Program): CLEP is the College-Level Examination Program that provides students with the opportunity to demonstrate college-level achievement through a program of exams in undergraduate college courses. There are 2,900 colleges that grant credit and/or advanced standing for CLEP exams. Each college publishes its qualifying criteria and number of credits awarded for CLEP exams. The qualifying criteria and credits awarded will vary by college.

COA (Cost of Attendance): The cost of attendance represents tuition, fees, room and board, books and supplies, travel and incidental expenses. The COA is compared to a student's EFC to determine the student's need for aid:

COA - EFC = student's financial need

College: Though the term "college" is commonly used to describe many types of postsecondary education, it is also used to describe a particular kind or subset of educational institution. "College" can be used to distinguish solely undergraduate institutions from those which also maintain graduate programs. Within a given school, its "colleges" may be its areas of study, like the "College of Arts and Sciences" or the "College of Architecture."

College Board: The College Board is a not-for-profit organization that administers many standardized tests including the PSAT, SAT I, SAT II, and AP tests. You will register with the College Board when you take any of these tests. Additionally, the College Board offers official test prep materials, a scholarship search, a personal inventory tool, and educational loans. You can find out more information about the college board at *www. collegeboard.com.*

Commencement: Also known as graduation. A ceremony during which colleges award certificates and degrees to graduating students.

Commercial Loans: Commercial loans, also known as private or alternative loans, are available through several financial services providers. To qualify, you must pass a credit check, and the interest rate will be higher than that of a Direct or FFEL Stafford or Perkins loan. For these reasons, it is wise to investigate such low-interest, federally-sponsored options before applying for a commercial loan. In addition, beware of scholarship scams that are simply commercial loans in disguise.

Common Application: Sponsored by the National Association of Secondary School Principals (NASSAP), the Common Application is accepted by over 240 colleges. If you are applying to two or more of the colleges/universities that use the Common Application, it may be worth your while to use it. You fill out one application and submit it to all the schools you're interested in, with the appropriate application fees for each school. Some schools have a supplementary form that has to be filled out as well. If you're applying online, check to make sure each college has received a complete application. You can find out more information and apply online at *www. common.app.org.*

Community College: Also known as a "junior" or "two-year" college. These schools provide college courses for recent high school graduates and adults in their communities. Community colleges generally have fewer admissions requirements than four-year institutions and courses typically cost less than comparable courses at four-year schools. Most community colleges award two-year associates degrees, though some are now awarding bachelor's degrees. Many students use community college as a springboard to a four-year college or university. Some community colleges have established relationships with four-year universities called "Matriculation Agreements" that allow students easy transfer of credits and preferred admissions status.

Commuter College: A college where less than half of the students live on campus.

Commuter Student: A student who does not live on campus; typically "commuter" refers to a student living at home with his or her parents, but can also mean any student who lives off-campus.

Concentration: A concentration is a grouping of courses in a certain area like sports management or global economics. Concentrations are generally offered as supplements to majors or minors and as such require fewer courses than either. When investigating schools, it can be helpful to look over their lists of majors, minors and concentrations in order to make sure that a good number of courses in your areas of interest are offered.

Conditional Acceptance: An admissions status that is conditional upon a student fulfilling certain requirements either prior, or subsequent to, gaining college admission. Such requirements may include taking and passing additional classes prior to college enrollment, demonstrating English proficiency, or maintaining a certain minimum number of classes and GPA during the first year of college classes.

Consortium: A group of colleges or universities, usually in geographic proximity to each other, which share programs, libraries, facilities, and social events. Knowing that a college is a member of a consortium will provide you with the information on many opportunities available to the students.

Contact Period: Recruiters of student-athletes may make in-person and/or off-campus contacts and evaluations.

Co-op: Cooperative education (co-op) integrates classroom study with paid, supervised work experiences. These jobs are part- or full-time and may lead to academic credit.

Cooperative Education: In a cooperative education program, students spend time engaged in employment related to their major field of study in addition to their regular classroom experience. In some programs, students may attend classes full-time for six months and then work full-time in their area of study for six months.

Credit (or Credit Hour): The unit of measurement some institutions give for fulfilling course requirements.

CSS (College Scholarship Service): The division of the College Board which is responsible for the PROFILE form and the needs analysis which determines the family's contribution toward payment of a student's education.

CSS Profile (College Scholarship Service Financial Aid Profile): The CSS asks more about assets and investments than the FAFSA. The CSS profile generally calculates a higher EFC than the FAFSA. About 800 colleges require incoming freshman to complete the CSS Profile. These colleges use the information on the CSS Profile to help the director of financial aid determine how much of a discount from the cost of tuition, room, and board a student should receive.

CTBS (Comprehensive Tests of Basic Skills): In some school districts students in second, fourth, fifth, sixth, seventh, and eighth grades take the CTBS each spring. The CTBS is a norm-referenced test, which assesses individual student achievement in the areas of reading, language, mathematics, science, and social studies. Because it is a norm-referenced test, individual student achievement is compared with that of other students nationally who are in the same grade. Schools use the results from this test, in combination with other classroom assessments, to identify strengths and weaknesses of individual students in each of the areas tested.

Dead Period: Recruiters of student-athletes may write letters or make telephone calls; however, they cannot make in-person contact or evaluations on or off campus or permit official or unofficial visits.

Decile: A division of 10ths used to rank students; the top decile is the top 10 percent, and the second decile is a student who ranks in the second 10 percent of his class.

Default: Failure to repay a loan according to the terms agreed to when you signed a promissory note.

Deferral: A decision regarding an early decision or early action student about whom an admission decision will be made during the regular decision period. If you're deferred in December, the college will typically notify you in April/May of a decision.

Deferred: A decision regarding your admission is being postponed. You may be required to take additional courses, provide additional information, or be given other reasons that the college will state in their letter to you.

Demonstrated Need: The formula that takes the total annual cost of attending college and subtracts the student's EFC to arrive at the amount the student will need to pay for college.

Deny: You were not accepted into this college at this time.

Division I (I-A and I-AA): Division I schools have at least seven sports for men, and seven for women, with two team sports for each gender.

- Division I schools must play 100 percent of the minimum number of contests against Division I opponents (there is an exception for football and basketball).

- Division I basketball teams have to play all but two games against Division I teams and must play 1/3 of all their contests in the home arena.

- Division I-A football programs must meet minimum attendance requirements.

- Division I-AA teams do not have minimum attendance requirements.

Division II: Division II schools have at least four sports for men and four for women, with two team sports for each gender, and each playing season represented by each gender. Football and basketball teams must play at least 50 percent of their games against Division II, I-A, or I-AA opponents.

Division III: Division III schools have to sponsor at least five sports for men and five for women, with two team sports for each gender, and each playing season represented by each gender. ***Division III schools cannot award athletic scholarships.***

Division III Exception: Currently the NCAA qualifying requirements do not apply to Division III colleges. Student eligibility for financial aid, practice, and competition is governed by institutional, conference and other NCAA regulations.

Double Major: Allows a student to complete two college major fields of study simultaneously.

DRN (Data Release Number): A four-digit number, located in the lower left corner of the first page of the SAR. Students need this number to apply to additional schools.

Dual Enrollment: Programs established between high schools with local colleges that allow students to earn college credit while still in high school.

Early Action: An Early Action program has earlier deadlines and earlier notification dates than the regular admissions process. Unlike the Early Decision program, the Early Action program does not require that a student commit to attending the school if admitted.

Early Action (Single-Choice): This program works like a combination of Early Action and Early Decision. Like Early Action, students are not obligated to attend the school if accepted, however, like Early Decision, students may only apply to one school under the Single-Choice Early Action program.

Early Admission: Procedure used by colleges that allows gifted high school juniors to skip their senior year and enroll instead in college. The term "Early Admission" is sometimes used to refer collectively to Early Action and Early Decision programs.

Early Decision: Some colleges offer the option of an early decision to students who meet all entrance requirements, are certain of the college they wish to attend and are likely to be accepted by that college. Students participate in the Early Decision plan by indicating their desire to participate on their college application. The decision regarding admission is made by mid-December of the student's 12th year in high school, as opposed to the regular admissions notification of mid-April. A drawback of the Early Decision program is that students will have to commit to a school before they find out about the financial-aid package.

A student can apply Early Decision to only one school.

Early Decision II: This policy is offered by some schools as a second round of Early Decision, usually with a January deadline.

EFC (Expected Family Contribution): The federal government uses the data you supply on the FAFSA to determine your estimated family contribution. This is the amount your family can afford to pay for college tuition. The EFC serves as a baseline to help the college estimate how much you can pay, how much more you'll need, and how much financial aid you are eligible to receive. There are two methods used to determine your EFC (i.e., federal and institutional).

CPO - EFC = Financial Need

Electronic Applications: An alternative to traditional paper applications, electronic applications can take several forms. Some schools allow you to print from their web site or a CD-ROM, application forms which you can fill in by hand and send to the admissions office. Other schools support online applications that you can fill out and submit over the Internet. If you decide to apply electronically, you will not have to wait to receive materials in the mail and you may even save some postage. Best of all, applying electronically will get your application in the hands of admissions officers that much sooner.

EOCT (End-of-Course-Test): A test that is administered to assess students' subject-area knowledge.

EOG (End-of-Grade): A test that is administered to assess students' knowledge within a specific subject area or across a broad range of subjects.

Equivalency Sports: All sports other than "Head Count" sports. Generally, this means that one full grant-in-aid (full ride) can be divided among more than one student-athlete. Note that all Division II sports are considered equivalency sports.

Evaluation Period: Recruiters of student-athletes can only assess academic qualifications and playing abilities. No in-person or off-campus recruiting contacts are permitted.

Exit Exam: Some states require that high school students pass one or more exit exams prior to students' being granted their high school diploma.

FAE (Financial Aid Estimator): About a month after receiving the SAR report, U.S. students will receive a financial-aid offer in the mail from the schools applied to. Many Division II and III colleges use an FAE to provide preliminary information from which they can estimate the amount of financial aid needed to attend their school.

FAFSA (Free Application for Federal Student Aid): The Free Application for Federal Student Aid (FAFSA) is used to apply for financial aid, including grants, loans, and work-study. In addition, it is used by most states and schools to award non-federal student financial aid. The form is a snapshot of a family's financial situation including income, debt, assets, etc., for both the parents and the student. Families must complete the FAFSA every year that the student attends college. Many colleges award institutional grants (discounts from the announced tuition, room and board) and other financial aid based on the information generated by the FAFSA. When information from the FAFSA is used as a baseline for awarding financial aid, this formula is called **federal methodology.** When an institution uses its own unique formula for determining student need and consequently which students will receive tuition discounts, this is called **institutional methodology.** FAFSA information is available at *www.fafsa.ed.gov/* or by calling 1.800.4.FED.AID.

FAO (Financial Aid Officer): The college's financial aid officer applies the school's own methods in determining each award and can also factor in extenuating circumstances such as a recent job loss. The Financial Aid Officer will review the SAR and eventually interview the student. The FAO is the person at the college who ultimately makes the final decisions regarding a student's financial-aid package.

Federal Methodology: Federal Methodology is used by the government and public institutions.

Federal Student Aid Programs: Programs administered by the U.S. Department of Education:

- Federal Pell Grant
- Federal Supplemental Educational Opportunity Grant (SEOG)
- Federal Work-Study (FWS)
- Federal Perkins Loan
- Federal PLUS Loan (Federal Family Education Loan Program (FFELP))
- Federal Direct Consolidation Loan
- Federal Stafford Loan (Federal Family Education Loan Program (FFELP))

FCAT (Florida Comprehensive Assessment Test): The primary purpose of the FCAT is to assess student achievement of the high-order cognitive skills represented in the Sunshine State Standards (SSS) in Reading, Writing, Mathematics, and Science. The SSS portion of FCAT is a criterion-referenced test. A secondary purpose is to compare the performance of Florida students to the Reading and Mathematics performance of students across the nation using a norm-referenced test (NRT). All students in Grades 3-10 take the FCAT Reading and Mathematics in the spring of each year. All students in Grades 4, 8, and 10 take FCAT Writing and FCAT Science is administered to all students in Grades 5, 8, and 10.

Fellowships: Fellowships and scholarships are available to students in most disciplines. They are sponsored by colleges and a broad range of organizations and institutions. Fellowships offered by organizations are often allocated in monthly stipends and can usually be used at any university. Fellowships are more common at the graduate level, but some undergraduate fellowships do exist. Additionally, there may be grant and fellowship money available for specific research projects or study abroad. Contact your major department, financial-aid office, or career center for more information.

FFEL: Federal Family Education Loan (FFEL) Program Stafford Loans are low-interest education loans made by private lenders to students and parents. These loans may be either subsidized or unsubsidized and have several repayment options.

Financial Aid: The term "financial aid" is used to describe the combination of loans, scholarships, grants, and work-study that will help a student pay for college.

Freshman Fifteen: The extra weight gain—about 15 pounds—associated with freshman year.

FSAIC (Federal Student Aid Information Center): Federal department for questions about federal student aid call 800.433.3243.

FSEOG (or SEOG): Federal Supplemental Educational Opportunity Grants (FSEOG) are government-sponsored, college-administered loans awarded to exceptionally needy students. Eligibility for FSEOGs is determined by the federal government and the program gives priority to students receiving federal Pell Grants. FSEOGs are awarded by each school from available federal funds. There is no guarantee that each school will have enough funding to award an FSEOG to every eligible student.

GED: General Education Development Certificate is awarded after a student passes a specific, approved high school equivalency test.

GPA: Grade point average represents the numerical average of a student's course grades. Calculation may be based on numerical points assigned to individual grades, i.e., A=4, B=3, C=2, D=1, F=0 or the calculation may be based on the actual numerical points earned within each course, i.e., 94.3, 87.5, 77.7, etc.

Grant Aid: The most sought after type of financial aid, grant aid does not have to be paid back. You may receive grant aid on the basis of either need or merit, and it may come from your school or the federal government. Federal grants include the need-based Pell and Federal Supplemental Educational Opportunity (FSEOG) grants.

Greek System: The common governing body for fraternities and sororities. These organizations vary in their role, size, mission, and traditions from college to college. First and foremost, they act as a social outlet from the rigors of intensive study. These organizations have espoused high ideals of friendship and service since the founding of Phi Beta Kappa in 1776.

Half Time: At schools measuring progress in credit hours and semesters, trimesters, or quarters, "half time" is at least six semester hours or quarter hours per term for an undergraduate program. A student must be attending school at least half time to be eligible for certain types of financial aid.

HBCUs (Historical Black Colleges and Universities): 98 colleges and universities as defined by the amended Higher Education Act of 1965 as any historically black college or university that was established prior to 1964, whose principal mission was, and is, the education of black Americans, and that is accredited by a nationally recognized accrediting agency or association determined by the Secretary [of Education] to be a reliable authority as to the quality of training offered or is, according to such an agency or association, making reasonable progress toward accreditation. For a listing of HBCUs go to the U.S. Department of Education web site at *www.ed.gov/about/inits/list/whhbcu/edlite-list.html.*

Head Count Limits: Represents the maximum number of athletic scholarships per Division I sport. For example:

- I-A Football: 85
- I-AA Football: 63
- Men's Basketball: 13
- Ice Hockey: 30

- Women's Basketball: 15
- Women's Gymnastics: 12
- Women's Tennis: 8
- Women's Volleyball: 12

Head Count Sports: Used for some Division I sports. Any athlete who receives institutional financial aid, no matter the amount, is counted as one. Head count limit sports exist in Division I only.

High School Schedules:

Traditional Schedule: A traditional 6-8 period schedule is the traditional Carnegie-unit-oriented schedule. Students usually have six to eight class periods during the school day that last for the entire school year and result in the awarding of one Carnegie unit. Elective classes may rotate for 9 or 18 week sessions, which earn .25 or .5 Carnegie units for each session. Schools that have traditional 6-8 period schedules usually have 45-55 minute class periods.

Block Schedule: The block schedule has fewer classes than a traditional 6-8 period schedule. Usually class times are longer and the schedule is accelerated to cover more material. Customarily, each ninety-minute period meets for ninety days in a semester to cover one academic year's worth of content credits (Carnegie units).

Intensive Block: In this format, students attend two core classes at a time. These core classes can be coupled with up to three other year-long elective classes. Students complete the core classes in 60 days and then move on to another two. School years are organized into trimesters.

4 x 4 Block: In this, the most common block schedule, the school day is divided into four 90-minute blocks. The school year is divided into two semesters, with four of what used to be year-long courses completed each semester. This format enables students to attend four classes per day, each lasting anywhere from 85-100 minutes. Students complete in one semester what would have taken them a full year in traditional schedules.

Alternating Plan (also known as the A/B plan): Like the 4 x 4 block schedule, the basic A/B plan organizes the school day into four 90-minute periods, but "A" days and "B" days have different classes, for a total of eight classes each semester. On an A/B schedule classes usually last for the entire year and earn one Carnegie unit.

75-75-30 Plan: With the 75-75-30 plan, the school year is divided into two 75-day terms followed by a 30-day term. Students take three courses during fall term and again during winter term. The spring term is frequently devoted to enrichment activities.

Copernican Plan: There are several variations of the Copernican plan. Students may attend blocked classes for 30, 45, 65 or 90 days, usually in the mornings. The afternoons are devoted to seminars and to the kinds of electives students typically want to take all year long.

Modified Block: These are usually variations of either the 4 x 4 or A/B plans. For example, a school might operate a A/B block schedule Monday through Thursday, and then have all eight classes meet for short periods on Friday. Or, they might have two 90-minute blocks every morning and three 60-minute blocks every afternoon. This is sort of a "build your own block schedule" format. For example, schools may have students attend school based on a 4 x 4 block on Monday through Thursday, and a regular eight-period schedule on Friday. Or, they might have two blocked classes in a day, combined with three regular periods.

Parallel Block: The parallel block is used primarily in elementary schools, whereas the previous four formats are used primarily in secondary schools. The Parallel block takes a class of students and divides them into two groups. One group of children stay with their classroom teacher for instruction in an academically demanding subject such as math or language arts, while the other group attends physical education or music, or visits the computer lab; after a prescribed length of time the two groups swap.

Hook: Refers to something contained in an admissions essay that engages the reader. Usually the "hook," is a unique personal trait or experience. For example, a student who has overcome a physical handicap, survived a high-poverty–high-crime community, participated in a disaster relief effort, or has visited another country as part of a humanitarian mission may refer to these experiences as a starting point for their college essays. A student's hook will be something about the student that's unique and interesting.

Hope Credit: A nonrefundable federal income tax credit equal to all of the first $1,000 "out-of-pocket" payments for qualified tuition and related expenses and 50 percent of the second $1,000, for a maximum $1,500 per student, per year. The Hope credit applies to the first two years of postsecondary education. You may not claim both the Hope Credit and the Lifetime Learning Credit for the same student.

Hope Scholarship: Available to Georgia residents who earn at least an 80 numeric average (college prep track) or 85 numeric average (vocational tech track) in the CORE curriculum (Language Arts, Math, Science, Social Studies & Foreign Language). HOPE assistance includes full-time tuition, approved mandatory fees, and a ($100-$150) book allowance, when attending a public college/university. At a private university, the HOPE scholarship is $3,000 per academic year. In addition, the student may qualify for the Georgia tuition Equalization Grant of $1,100. HOPE does not cover room and board and can only be used at a Georgia institution. HOPE is renewable if the student maintains a 3.0 GPA and attends full-time. More information is available at *www.gsfc.org*.

Humanities: Major grouping of subjects of study, e.g., Art History, English Literature, Languages, History, Music, Philosophy, and Religious Studies.

IB (International Baccalaureate): IB courses focus on critical thinking and writing and were designed to provide an international credential for university entrance. Like APs, IB courses can result in college credit and are considered more rigorous than standard courses. Some international high schools award IB diplomas upon the completion of a certain sequence of IB courses. IB tests are scored on a scale of 1-7 with 7 being best.

Institutional Methodology: Institutional Methodology is an alternate method typically used by a private college or university to determine a students' eligibility for scholarships and grants under their direct control.

Institutional Methodology requires completing a CSS Profile form, which is processed by the College Board. The tax year before a student enrolls in college is the year that will be analyzed to determine a student's aid eligibility. This is called the base income year, and it's a crucial period because it sets the tone for the types of financial-aid packages that a student can expect throughout the college years (though you will have to reapply every year). Institutional Methodology almost always increases the student's EFC. The Institutional Methodology tends to include additional assets like home equity that aren't included on the FAFSA. When these additional assets are added, the student's EFC will increase. The school then takes this new EFC, subtract it from the "Cost of Attendance" (COA) to determine how much assistance the student needs. If the student's Institutional EFC is higher, the amount of assistance is lower, and the student ends up paying more.

International Student: A student who is not a U.S. citizen and does not live in the United States.

Internships: Part-time or full-time opportunities to gain professional work experience while in college. Some interns are paid, while others receive college credit. Either way, the experience is invaluable to a student looking for employment after college.

ITBS (Iowa Tests of Basic Skills): Developed by the University of Iowa, the ITBS is given to students in grades 3-8 and the Iowa Tests of Educational Development (ITED) is given to students in grades 9 and 11. These tests are norm-referenced, standardized tests. Norm-referenced means that the test compares individual student performance with the performance of other students (in the state or national reference group) in the same grade, taking the test at the same time of year. These tests then rank order the students. ITBS/ITED are also standardized, which means that they are administered to all test takers in the same way under the same conditions. The national average score is 50, and is based upon a national sample selected from 1995.

ITED (Iowa Tests of Educational Development): *See ITBS.*

Ivy League: The athletic conference that boasts eight of the country's foremost academic universities:

1. Brown
2. Columbia
3. Cornell
4. Dartmouth
5. Harvard
6. Penn
7. Princeton
8. Yale

Admissions into an Ivy League school is among the most competitive in the United States.

Joint Enrollment: *See Dual Enrollment.*

Lab Sciences: High school science courses that supplement textbook study with hands-on experimentation. Examples include biology, chemistry, and physics. Other courses, such as economics, may be considered scientific disciplines, but do not qualify as lab sciences. Consult your guidance counselor or your prospective college's admissions office for further details.

Legatee: A student whose parent graduated from the college's undergraduate school.

Lifetime Learning Credit: The Lifetime Learning Credit may be claimed for the qualified tuition and related expenses of the students in the taxpayer's family who are enrolled in eligible educational institutions. Through 2002, the amount that may be claimed as a credit is equal to 20 percent of the taxpayer's first $5,000 of out-of-pocket qualified tuition and related expenses for all the students in the family for a maximum of $1,000. Individuals with modified adjusted gross incomes of $50,000 or more and joint filers with modified adjusted gross incomes of $100,000 or more are not eligible for the Lifetime Learning Credit.

Liberal Arts: Courses of study providing a broad range of exposure in the arts, natural sciences, social sciences, and humanities.

Magnet School: A public school with a specialized or unique focus.

Major: A concentration of courses (usually around 9 or 10) in a specialized field of study.

Minority: For admissions purposes, a minority is someone who is black, Hispanic, or indigenous. For reporting purposes, colleges typically include those of Asian heritage and sometimes international students.

"Match" School: A college where a student has a 75 percent chance of being accepted.

Merit-Based Aid: In general terms, merit-based aid is any form of financial aid not based on demonstrated financial need. Merit-based aid, which can take the form of grants, scholarships, or loans on favorable terms, is generally granted by each school and/or its alumni associations and wealthy benefactors. A student may qualify for merit-based aid by meeting certain academic requirements, such as grade point average or test scores, or for aspiring toward certain career goals. Alternatively, a student may qualify through an essay competition. The financial-aid package may include both need- and merit-based aid.

Minor: A concentration of courses in a field of study other than the major.

NACDA (National Association of College Directors of Athletics): The National Association of College Directors lists the names and addresses of all the coaches in the United States. Contact 216.835.1172 for more information.

NAIA (National Association of Intercollegiate Athletics): The NAIA revolutionized national collegiate athletics by becoming the first organization to offer collegiate athletics to both men and women with the establishment of athletic programs for women on August 1, 1980. The championship calendar for women began that year with basketball, cross country, gymnastics, indoor and outdoor track and field, softball, tennis and volleyball. Soccer was added in 1984, and golf was included in 1995.

National Achievement Scholarship: The National Achievement^{SM} Scholarship Program is an academic competition established in 1964 to provide recognition for outstanding Black American high school students. Black students may enter both the National Achievement Program and the National Merit® Program by taking the PSAT/ NMSQT® and meeting other published requirements for participation. The two annual programs are conducted simultaneously but operated and funded separately.

A student's standing is determined independently in each program. Black American students can qualify for recognition and be honored as Scholars in both the National Merit® Program and the National Achievement Program, but can receive only one monetary award from NMSC.

National Merit Scholarship: A distinction awarded upon the basis of a U.S. high school junior's score on the NMSQT/PSAT (National Merit Scholar Qualifying Test/Preliminary Scholastic Aptitude Test). Those scoring at or above a certain level are eligible to apply for a limited number of National Merit Scholarships.

The test may be administered for practice during the student's sophomore year, but only the junior year score counts.

NCAA (National Collegiate Athletic Association): Founded in 1906, the NCAA is made up of 977 schools classified in three divisions:

- Division I: 321 schools

- Division II: 260 schools

- Division III: 396 schools

The NCAA sponsors 87 championships in 22 sports, including the highly-publicized Final Four in men and women's basketball. Almost 24,500 men and women student-athletes compete annually for NCAA titles.

NCAA Clearinghouse: U.S. high school student-athletes who want to be eligible to compete as college freshman in athletic competition must register with the NCAA Clearinghouse. The only exception is for those students who have been home-schooled during all of grades 9 through 12.

The best time to register is after the student's junior, but before the student's senior year, when junior year grades appear on the student's transcript.

A student can get the necessary forms from their counselor, by calling the NCAA Clearinghouse at 877.262.1492 or at *www.ncaaclearinghouse.net.*

NACAC (National Association for College Admission Counseling): Founded in 1937, the NACAC is an organization of 8,000 professionals from around the world dedicated to serving students as they make choices about pursuing postsecondary education. NACAC is committed to maintaining high standards that foster ethical and social responsibility among those involved in the transition process. Go to *www.nacac.com* for more information.

Need-Based Aid: If the Cost of Attendance (COA) exceeds a student's Expected Family Contribution (EFC), the student will be eligible for need-based aid to cover the difference. A financial-aid package may consist of a combination of grants, scholarships, loans, and work-study. The total amount of a student's financial-aid package will be determined by a combination of demonstrated financial need, federal award maximums, and the school's available funds.

Need-Blind Admissions: The ability of an applicant to pay does not affect the college's consideration of his/her application.

Need-Conscious Admission: Due to tight money and limited financial aid, some colleges consider a student's "ability to pay" in the admission decision.

Needs Analysis: The process used to evaluate an applicant's financial situation to determine how much student aid he or she needs to help meet postsecondary educational expenses.

NJCAA (National Junior College Athletic Association): The idea for the NJCAA was conceived in 1937 at Fresno, California. A handful of junior college representatives met to organize an association that would promote and supervise a national program of junior college sports and activities consistent with the educational objectives of junior colleges. The NJCAA, which now has 503 member schools in 42 states, is the national governing body of 15 men's and 12 women's sports over three divisions. Approximately 45,300 athletes compete for 50 national championships in 24 regions.

NMSQT (National Merit Scholarship Qualifying Test): When the PSAT is taken during a high school student's junior year, the scores are used to qualify for national Merit Scholarships. Students with scores in the top 5 percent nationally, receive Letters of Commendation. Students with scores in the top 1.5 percent are National merit Semifinalists and may compete for scholarships of $2,000 or more.

Online Applications: Online applications are a specific type of electronic application. When students use an online application, they submit personal and academic information to the school over a secure Internet site. A student will, however, probably be required to supplement their online application with hard copies of their transcript, letters of recommendation, etc.

Open Admissions: Students are admitted regardless of academic qualifications. The school may require an additional probationary period during which the student must earn satisfactory grades to ensure continued enrollment.

Orientation: Most schools offer orientation for incoming students to help ease the transition into college. During orientation (which can last a couple of days to over a week) students have the opportunity to participate in a variety of programs and information sessions that allow them to experience a small taste of what their undergraduate years will be like.

Out-of-State Student: This term generally applies to students applying to a public college or university. Tuition rates are lower for state residents; out-of-state students must pay a higher rate of tuition until they have established the legal residency requirements for the state.

Partial Qualifier: Under the NCAA guidelines certain student-athletes qualify as partial qualifiers. They cannot compete in contests or events but are eligible to practice with a team at its home facility and receive an athletic scholarship during their first year at a Division I school and then have three seasons of qualification for competition.

Pell Grants: Given by the Federal Government, these grants are awarded to those students demonstrating exceptional financial need. Pell grants do not need to be paid back.

Perkins Loans: Awarded by the student's school, these low-interest loans (.5 percent) are given to students (both undergraduate and graduate) that demonstrate exceptional financial need. Repayment of this loan begins nine months after the student graduates, leave school or drop to less than half-time student status.

PG Year: Post-graduate year attended after graduating high school; usually completed at a prep school in order to compete in sports or improve grades.

PLUS (Parent Loans for Undergraduate Students): This is an unsubsidized federal loan for parents or legal guardians of dependent undergraduate students. This loan allows parents to borrow all or some of the difference between financial aid received and the cost of attending the school, including room, board, and other charges. The PLUS is not based on need, so the FAFSA is not required.

Preferential Aid Package: A process by which colleges award better financial-aid packages to more desirable applicants.

Presidential Scholar: The United States Presidential Scholars Program was established in 1964, by Executive Order of the President, to recognize and honor our nation's most distinguished high school students. In 1979, the program was extended to recognize students who demonstrate exceptional talent in the visual, creative, and performing arts.

Each year, 141 high school seniors are named Presidential Scholars. These students are chosen on the basis of academic and artistic success, leadership, and involvement in school and community affairs.

There are two ways to become a Presidential scholar. One hundred twenty-one scholars are chosen on the basis of "broad academic achievement." Twenty students are selected as arts scholars, on the basis of excellence in visual, performing, or creative arts, in addition to scholastic achievement.

Private Counselors: You may consult private counselors as you prepare to select and apply to colleges. They may operate as consultants or as employees of educational service providers such as Kaplan or the Princeton Review. Private counselors can help students assess their personality and academic needs to form a list of desirable college attributes. They can also assist students in figuring out where and to how many schools they should apply to.

PROFILE: *See CSS/Financial Aid PROFILE.*

Promissory Note: The binding legal document that is signed when acquiring a student loan. It is very important to read and save this document because it will be referred to at a later date when the student begins repaying the loan.

PSAT/NMSQT (Preliminary SAT ®/National Merit Scholarship Qualifying Test): PSAT/NMSQT stands for Preliminary SAT/National Merit Scholarship Qualifying Test. It's a standardized test that provides firsthand practice for the SAT I: Reasoning Test. It also gives students a chance to enter the National Merit Scholarship Corporation (NMSC) scholarship programs. The PSAT/NMSQT measures: verbal reasoning skills; critical reading skills; math problem-solving skills; and writing skills.

A perfect score is 80.

Quartile/Quintile: A division of fourths or fifths used to rank students; the top quartile is the top 25 percent, and the second quintile is a student who ranks in the second 20 percent of his class.

Quiet Period: Recruiters of student-athletes may make telephone calls, write letters, and make in-person contact only on the college campus.

Rank: *See Class Rank.*

"Reach" School: A college where the applicant has a 25 percent or less chance of acceptance.

Registration: Registering on time is an important part of doing your best on admissions tests. Generally, registration involves filling out a form with your personal information, indicating your testing site preferences, and submitting a fee. Register as early as possible and you'll have a good chance of getting your first-choice test site. Consult the College Board, ACT web site, or your guidance counselor at least two months before your desired test date to begin the process.

Regular Student: Refers to a student who is enrolled or accepted for enrollment at an institution for the purpose of obtaining a degree, certificate, or other recognized educational credential offered by that institution.

Remediation: Students who are not fully prepared for college academically are often required to complete remedial classes. The courses are designed to bring the student up to the level required for satisfactory college-level performance. Such courses are usually not granted credit towards graduation.

Residential Campus: A college that provides (or requires) on-campus housing for most or all students. Many colleges require all first-year students to live in college housing.

Residential College: Has two meanings: (1) a college at which more than 50 percent of the students live on campus, usually a college at which more than 75 percent of the students live on campus; (2) a residential organization within a larger college, often of 200-600 students. Yale is the father of the "residential college" system, whereby students are assigned to a smaller college within Yale (such as Berkeley) and typically live in that college during their four years at Yale. Helps to make the college experience more personal and diminishes the need for fraternities.

Résumé: A 4-year list of work, extracurricular, and award experiences that will be used for college and scholarship applications.

Rolling Admissions: Students' applications are considered when all required credentials have been submitted. There is either no deadline or a very late deadline; qualified students are accepted until classes are filled. Applicants are notified of admission continuously throughout the enrollment period.

Room and Board: The cost of the dormitory room and meal plan.

ROTC (Reserve Officers' Training Corps): A program that allows students to earn a college degree and an officer's commission at the same time. Upon graduation, the student serves in a branch of the military.

"Safety" School: A college where the student has a 90-100 percent chance of being accepted.

Salutatorian: The second-ranked student in a graduating class.

SAR (Student Aid Report): The SAR is generated by the U.S. Department of Education and is based on the information provided on the FAFSA. In the lower left corner of the first page of the SAR will be a four-digit number. This is the DRN (Data Release Number). Students will need this number to apply to additional schools.

The college's financial-aid office will calculate (federal methodology) the federal and state financial aid available to students from the EFC number and other information of the SAR.

SAT I (also called the SAT Reasoning Test): The Standard Aptitude Test (SAT) is administered by the College Board. The SAT uses multiple choice questions to assess reading and mathematical reasoning ability. The SAT is usually taken by college-bound high school students during their 11th and/or 12th years.

Prior to 2005, the top score was 1600, 800 for the Math and 800 for the Verbal.

The top score for the new SAT I is 2400. 800 for Math, 800 for Critical Reading (replaces Verbal), and 800 for Writing.

SAT II: The SAT IIs assess knowledge in various high school subject areas. Most colleges require some version of the Math test and a foreign language test. Even colleges that do not require the SAT IIs will usually review the scores as additional info about a student's abilities. Students usually take these tests in the spring of their junior year and the fall of their senior year.

If the test is linked to a specific subject like Chemistry, it's best to take the test as soon as possible upon the completion of the course.

SAT-9 (Stanford Achievement Tests 9th Edition): The Stanford Achievement Test Series, 9th Edition, not to be confused with the Scholastic Aptitude Test (also SAT) is a combination of multiple-choice and open-ended subtests for grades K-12.

Scholarships: A type of financial aid which does not require repayment or employment and is usually awarded to students who demonstrate or show potential for achievement—usually academic—at that institution.

Score Choice: A student may withhold SAT II scores from colleges. If a student chooses score choice the student must go through the process of "releasing" their scores to colleges.

Selective Admissions: Admissions procedure used by colleges and universities, where additional standards and criteria are required. Usually for specific programs or departments.

SEOG (Student Educational Opportunity Grant): *See FSEOG.*

Single-Choice Early Action: *See Early Action (Single-Choice)*

Social Sciences: Major grouping of similar subjects, e.g. Psychology, Sociology, Political Science, Economics, and Geography.

Squeeze Play: A student uses an offer of admission from one college to force an early offer from another school. Early offers of admission, are often accompanied by generous financial aid awards, and are usually only given to recruited applicants.

SRF (Student Release Form): A Student Release Form (SRF) must be completed and submitted to the NCAA Clearinghouse to allow access to your high school transcript.

SSR (Secondary School Report): A report from the student's high school that provides such information as student transcript, class rank, discipline information, and other pertinent information about the student and student's high school.

Stafford Loans: These loans, both subsidized (need-based) and unsubsidized (non-need-based), are guaranteed by the federal government and available to students to fund education. Federal Stafford Loans are the most common source of education loan funds. They are available to both graduate and undergraduate students. *See also Direct Loans and FFEL.*

Student-Athlete: A student who plays or is planning to compete in a college-level sport.

Study Abroad: While in college, many students choose to spend time studying in a foreign country. During their stay there, students are immersed in the culture, history, and academic-life of their chosen destination.

Subsidized/Unsubsidized Loans: Subsidized loans are based upon financial need. With these loans, the interest is paid by the government until the repayment period begins and during authorized periods of deferment afterwards. Unsubsidized loans are not need-based, so all students are eligible to receive them. Interest payments begin immediately on unsubsidized loans, although you can waive the payments and the interest will be capitalized.

Syllabus: Course requirements given out by the instructor. Includes detailed information about the course, such as the grading scale, attendance policies, testing, and assignment dates.

TA (Teaching Assistant): Most often a graduate student, who will teach discussion sections of large lecture classes. Used most often at larger universities.

TerraNova CTBS ™: TerraNova is a norm-referenced achievement test that compares students' scores to scores from a "norm group." The norm group for TerraNova is a U.S. national sample of students representing all gender, racial, economic, and geographic groups.

Test Prep: Books, videos, CD-ROMs, and classroom courses designed to assist a student in preparing for such tests as the SAT I, SAT II, ACT, and PSAT. It is wise to do some sort of prep, if only looking over the informational packet about each test to familiarize yourself with the number and type of questions you'll be expected to answer.

TOEFL (Test of English as a Foreign Language): Used as a national test for college admission and placement for students who have English as a second language and whose scores on the SAT I might not reflect their potential for higher education because of inexperience with the English language.

Transcript: A student's high school academic record. The student's guidance counselor or school registrar compiles this listing of all courses, grades, and standardized test scores. A college will likely ask for official copies of a student's transcript, which is usually signed across the seal by the appropriate school official and should not be opened.

Transfer: The process of transferring from a community college to a four-year university or from one four-year university to another four-year university. Transferring can be a tricky process, especially when it comes time to figure out how many of a student's previously earned credits will count at the new school. To make the transition as simple as possible, a student should request application materials from prospective schools as early as possible and figure out how credits will be accounted for BEFORE beginning the transfer process.

Transfer Credit: Course credit that is accepted from or by another college or university. Usually college level credits with a grade of "C" or better.

Tuition: The cost of attending college classes.

University: Though it is common to use the term "college" to describe all postsecondary schools, a student may be applying to universities as well as colleges. There can be some important differences: Universities generally support both undergraduate and graduate programs and tend to be larger than colleges. Many universities are comprised of colleges that represent undergraduate and graduate programs, and/or specialized areas of study.

Valedictorian: The top-ranked student in a graduating class.

Viewbook: A college's sales brochure.

Virtual Tour: An online college tour that can be viewed on some college web sites.

Wait List: Being placed on a wait list indicates that a student has not been denied admissions to a college but their admissions status is on hold until those students who have been admitted make their decision. If a student has been placed on a waiting list, they will be notified if a place becomes available.

Waiver of View Recommendations: A practice whereby the student waives the right to see the recommendation letters. This is a customary practice so that teachers and counselors feel free to express honesty in their recommendation letters.

Weighted-GPA: Some high school honors, AP (Advanced Placement), AT (Academically Talented), GT (Gifted and Talented), and/or IB (International Baccalaureate) classes add points to grades to reflect their unusual level of difficulty. If you have taken such courses, your GPA may be considered weighted. Some colleges convert weighted GPAs to standard GPAs for the purposes of comparison.

Westinghouse: A competition for high school students. The finalist award is given to a few students each year who have completed outstanding scientific research; this is perhaps the most notable award a high school student can earn and is highly regarded by all colleges.

Who's Who: A for-profit company that publishes books listing students from throughout the country.

Yield: The percentage of accepted candidates who decide to enroll in a college. Because no college will have 100 percent yield, all selective colleges will send letters of acceptance to more students than they actually can enroll.

References

ACT. http://www.act.org/aap/

Bauld, H. (2001). *On Writing The College Application Essay: Secrets of a Former Ivy League Admissions Officer.* New York, NY: Harper & Row.

Boyer, Ernest L. (1983). *High School: A Report on Secondary Education in America.* New York, NY: Harper & Row.

Carnegie Foundation for the Advancement of Teaching. (1906). *First Annual Report.* October 15, 1906.

Cassidy, D. (2003). *The Scholarship Book 2003.* New York, NY: Prentice Hall Press.

Cohen, K. (2003). *Rock Hard Apps: How to Write a Killer College Application.* New York, NY: Hyperion Books.

College Board. http://www.collegeboard.org

Conley, David T. (2005). *College Knowledge: What it Really Takes for Students to Succeed and What We Can Do to Get Them Ready.* San Francisco, CA: Jossey-Bass.

Dunn, R., & Dunn, K. (1992). *Teaching Elementary Students Through Their Individual Learning Styles.* Boston, MA: Allyn & Bacon.

Dunn, R., & Dunn, K. (1993). *Teaching Secondary Students Through Their Individual Learning Styles: Practical Approaches for Grades 7-12.* Boston, MA: Allyn & Bacon.

Dunn, R., Dunn, K. & Perrin, J. (1994). *Teaching Young Children Through Their Individual Learning Styles.* Boston MA: Allyn & Bacon.

Dunn, R., & Dunn, K. (1999). *The Complete Guide to the Learning Styles Inservice System.* Boston, MA: Allyn & Bacon.

FastWeb. http://www.fastweb.com/

Gardner, Howard. (1983). *Frames of Mind: The Theory of Multiple Intelligences.* New York, NY: Harper and Row.

Get a Jump! What's Next After High School. (2003). Lawrenceville, NJ: Thomson-Peterson.

Hernandez, Michele A. (2000). *The Middle School Years: Achieving the Best Education for Your Child Grades 5-8.* New York, NY: Warner Books.

Kaplan, Ben. (2002). *How to Go to College Almost for Free.* New York, NY: HarperCollins.

Lagemann, Ellen Condliffe. (1983). *Private Power for the Public Good: A History of the Carnegie Foundation for the Advancement of Teaching.* Middletown, CT: Wesleyan University Press.

LaVeist, Thomas and Will. (2003). *8 Steps to Helping Black Families Pay for College.* New York, NY: The Princeton Review.

Lazear, David. (1991). *Seven Ways of Knowing: Teaching for Multiple Intelligences.* Palatine, IL: IRI/Skylight Publishing.

Mazzoni, Wayne. (1998). *The Athletic Recruiting & Scholarship Guide.* New York, NY: Mazz Marketing.

Montauk, R. and Klein, K. (2000). *How to Get into the Top Colleges.* New York, NY: Penquin Putnam.

Myers, Isabel Briggs and Myers, Peter. (1990). *Gifts Differing: Understanding Personality Type.* Palo Alto, CA: CPP Books.

NCAA Guide for the College Bound Student-Athlete. http://www.ncaa.org

Rubensteini, J. and Robinson, A. (2003). *Cracking the PSAT/NMSQT.* New York, NY: The Princeton Review.

Ruggiero, Vincent Ryan. (2001). *Beyond Feelings: A Guide to Critical Thinking.* Mountain View, CA: Mayfield Publishing Company.

SAT. http://www.collegeboard.com

Scholarships, Grants & Prizes, 2004. (2003). Lawrenceville, NJ: Thomson-Peterson.

Schwebel, S. (2001). *Yale Daily News Guide to Summer Programs.* Riverside, NJ: Simon & Schuster.

Student Services, Inc. (1997). *The B* Student's Complete Scholarship Book.* New York, NY: Sourcebooks.

TerraNova. http://www.ctb.com/mktg/terranova/tn_intro.jsp

Tanabe, Gen S. and Kelly Y. (2002). *Money-Winning Scholarship Essays and Interviews.* Los Altos, CA: SuperCollege.

U.S. Department of Education White Paper. (October 20, 1997). *Mathematics Equals Opportunity.* U.S. Department of Education.

U.S. News. http://www.usnews.com/usnews/home.htm

Wheeler, Dion. (2000). *A Parent's and Student-Athlete's Guide to Athletic Scholarships.* New York, NY: Contemporary Books.

Wynn, Mychal. (2005). *A High School Plan for Students with College-Bound Dreams.* Marietta, GA: Rising Sun Publishing.

Wynn, Mychal. (2005). *A Middle School Plan for Students with College-Bound Dreams.* Marietta, GA: Rising Sun Publishing.

Wynn, Mychal. (2001). *Follow Your Dreams: Lessons That I Learned in School.* Marietta, GA: Rising Sun Publishing.

Wynn, Mychal. (1990). *Don't Quit – Inspirational Poetry.* Marietta, GA: Rising Sun Publishing.

Wynn, Mychal. (2002). *Ten Steps to Helping Your Child Succeed in School.* Marietta, GA: Rising Sun Publishing.

Index

This Order May Be Placed By Mail • FAX • Telephone • E-mail
Payment May Be Made By Money Order • Check • Credit Card • Purchase Order

Enter the item number, description, corresponding price, and quantity for each selection (e.g., #5003, Follow Your Dreams, $7.95/ea.) and compute the total for that item. Shipping is 10% of the subtotal, (e.g, subtotal of $200.00 x .10 = $20.00 shipping charges). **Allow two weeks for processing.**

Item #	Description (Please Print)	Unit Price	X Quantity	= Total
6903	A High School Plan ... College-Bound Dreams	$ 19.95		
6905	A High School Plan ... *Workbook*	$15.95		
6901	A Middle School Plan ... College-Bound Dreams	$15.95		
6906	A Middle School Plan ... *Workbook*	$15.95		
5003	Follow Your Dreams	$ 7.95		
5001	Don't Quit	$ 9.95		
			`	

Method Of Payment
Do Not Send Cash • No C.O.D.s
❏ A check (payable to Rising Sun Publishing) is attached
❏ A purchase order is attached, P.O. # _____
Charge my: ❏ Visa ❏ Mastercard

_____
Account Number   Expiration Date

_____
Signature *(required for credit card purchases)*

SUBTOTAL $ _____

Shipping (Subtotal x 10%)   _____

Add Handling   3.50

Georgia residents
add 6% Sales Tax   _____

DATE: _____   TOTAL   _____

✉ Mail to:
RISING SUN PUBLISHING
P.O. Box 70906
Marietta, GA 30007-0906

RISING SUN
P U B L I S H I N G

☎ Phone toll-free: **1.800.524.2813**
FAX: **1.770.587.0862**
e-mail: orderdesk@rspublishing.com
web site: http://www.rspublishing.com

Ship to *(Please Print)* [Must be same as billing address for credit card purchases]:
Name _____
_____
Address _____
City_____ State_____ Zip _____
Day Phone (____) _____ Email : _____